Cultivating an Ethical School

Often the school as an institution is regarded as ethically neutral, leaving untouched questions about whether the school itself is a site of injustice toward both educators and children. Springing from his well-known *Building an Ethical School*, Robert J. Starratt now looks more closely at the educational leader's responsibility to ensure that the whole fabric of the educational process reflects an ethical philosophy of education.

Starratt argues that the work of educating young people is by its very nature an ethical work as well as an intellectual work, and that this work inescapably engages educators and their pupils with an academic curriculum, a social curriculum, and a civic curriculum. *Cultivating an Ethical School* lays a foundation for educators seeking to cultivate a comprehensive ethical educating environment. The second half of the book then takes up the more specific perspectives on teaching and learning that constitute the heart of cultivating an ethical school. Starratt provides examples of how an ethical school can expose students to a variety of perspectives on the challenges they will be called upon to face in the worlds of culture, nature, and society. This valuable book shows leaders and educators the importance of organizing a curriculum and a pedagogy that simultaneously respects and cultivates the intellectual, personal, and social qualities of being human.

Robert J. Starratt is Professor of Educational Leadership in the Lynch School of Education at Boston College. He received the Roald Campbell Lifetme Achievement Award in the field of Educational Administration, awarded by UCEA in 2006.

Cultivating an Ethical School

Robert J. Starratt

Routledge
Taylor & Francis Group

NEW YORK AND LONDON

First published 2012
by Routledge
711 Third Avenue, New York, NY 10017

Simultaneously published in the UK
by Routledge
2 Park Square, Milton Park, Abingdon, Oxon OX14 4RN

Routledge is an imprint of the Taylor & Francis Group, an informa business

© 2012 Taylor & Francis

The right of Robert J. Starratt to be identified as author of this work has been asserted by him in accordance with sections 77 and 78 of the Copyright, Designs and Patents Act 1988.

Library of Congress Cataloging in Publication Data
Starratt, Robert J.
    Cultivating an ethical school / Robert J. Starratt.
    p. cm.
    Includes bibliographical references and index.
    1. Moral education. 2. Education—Moral and ethical aspects. 3. Teachers—Professional ethics. I. Title.
    LC268.S69 2012
    370.11'4—dc23
    2011038874

ISBN: 978-0-415-88738-0 (hbk)
ISBN: 978-0-415-88739-7 (pbk)
ISBN: 978-0-203-83326-1 (ebk)

Typeset in Minion
by EvS Communication Networx, Inc.

Printed and bound in the United States of America on sustainably sourced paper by IBT Global

Contents

Preface

At the outset I should clarify the focus of this book and the standpoint I bring to that focus. The book attempts to present to educators and to educators of educators a process of teaching and learning and administering that opens up possibilities of transforming that work while respecting, nay, enriching the integrity of that work. The standpoint for developing that focus is the standpoint of ethics. The argument of the book is that the work of teaching and learning that goes on in schools has an ethical, as well as an intellectual, character to it and that the work of administering such a school has its own complementary ethical character. Furthermore, the argument boldly asserts that the cultivating of that ethical character draws out the true integrity of learning and teaching, without which learning, teaching, and administering lose their way.

In my graduate course on ethics and equity in education over the years, the vast majority of the students, even those who could recall a prior course in ethics, testified that they had never thought of education as intrinsically ethical work, or their work as administrators as so thoroughly ethical in nature. Most had read somewhere a document on the professional ethics of educators, but could not recall many details except that the statements were mainly framed as prohibitions—somewhat like the Ten Commandments in the Judeo-Christian tradition. Some were familiar with the phrase, "teaching (or working) for social justice," but were not able to elaborate much on its meaning, or the ethical reasoning behind that phrase. By the end of the course, however, most were more comfortable using the language and perspectives of ethics to analyze and interrogate situations at school that they had taken for granted, or that they felt no responsibility to actively resist.

It would appear that educators in the United States have, by and large, had minimal exposure to opportunities to think about, name, or enact their work as intrinsically ethical. This book is an attempt to delve deeply into the possibilities of intentionally engaging their work as ethical. The book, therefore, attempts to introduce ethical language and perspectives to audiences that by and large feel incapable of conversing about the ethical integrity of their work.

The book is not about character education, though it can be compatible with some forms of it. Neither is it a commentary on the loss of ethical character in American society and culture, though it may raise critical questions about some dispositions and practices in its institutional life. It is much more about the ethical possibilities of schooling, not only in the United States, but also in other countries. The book proposes that educators articulate and use ethical frameworks to imagine and cultivate positive ethical possibilities that flow from the very character of the learning agenda of schooling—whether in private, public, faith-based, or charter schools. In other words, the absence of inquiry and discussions about the intrinsically ethical character of school learning disables the necessary exploration of genuine possibilities of a transformed practice of teaching and learning.

The book invites the community of educators to reach for the "ideal type" of educating process, whose articulation can guide a realistic, on-the-ground journey toward the ideal, recognizing that its perfect achievement will always exceed their grasp, but also recognizing that, without that articulated ideal type, schooling will continue its haphazard and rudderless adventure under the fluctuating winds of the passionate politics of the moment. To be sure, that ideal type will need continuous interpretation as societies encounter changing historical circumstances.

Clarification of the Terms "Ethical" and "Moral"

It will help if at the outset I attempt to clarify my use of the terms ethical, ethics, ethician, on the one hand, and the terms moral, morality, moralist, and moralism. Some scholars distinguish between ethical and moral, claiming that the term moral refers to a type of behavior that is pre-ethical; that is, that being moral means behaving under the rules established by others, usually parents and adult authorities. In contrast, being ethical refers to behaving in ways consistent with internal, self-appropriated principles that one can articulate and that, at least sometimes, lead persons to go beyond self-interest. Using that distinction, moral persons behave in certain ways because that's what others demand and expect. Ethical persons behave in certain ways because they are convinced that it is the right thing to do, because doing the right thing is tied up with their identity (Conn, 1977). Others simply acknowledge the divide between a morality of obedience and a morality of personal integrity, without getting involved in the distinction between ethics and morality (Damon, 1984; Blasi, 1984).

I often use the adjectives "moral" and "ethical" interchangeably since they both are adjectives commonly used to describe activities or persons. Most of the time, when I use the adjective, "ethical," I also mean to imply that its referent, besides being moral, can articulate a reason or principle for claiming it to be moral.

I use the term "ethics," on the other hand, as a formal category of philosophical thinking. Thus I can refer to Aristotle's, Plato's, or Kant's "ethics" which was their philosophical attempt to probe the intelligibility of ethical actions and ethical persons. On the other hand, the term "morals" normally does not refer to the study of what constitutes morality.

I would tend to distinguish the term "ethician" or "ethicist" from the term "moralist" by saying that the term ethician or ethicist refers to someone—usually a philosopher—who attempts to explain the intelligibility of moral behavior or choices in both general and in particular situations, whereas the term moralist signifies for me a person who moralizes about moral behavior/choices—that is, one who tends to advocate for or preach about moral behavior/choices, sometimes employing a rather pedantic rhetoric with paternalistic, religious, or legal overtones.

What Hat Am I Wearing, Anyway?

For close to twenty years now I have taken up ethical issues around educational leadership, including this current effort. However, I do not consider myself an ethician or an ethicist. Rather, I consider myself an educator whose scholarship explores the intelligibility and legitimizing principles of the practice of educating. I go to the philosophers to gain a deeper and clearer understanding of ethics and the ways I might interpret educational activity as ethical. Because philosophers also take up the intelligibility of knowing or the intelligibility of meaning making, I also consult them to understand some foundational issues about the activity of learning. Philosophers also probe the intelligibility of what is particularly human. Reading and reflecting on what philosophers have to say about the intelligibility of being human, i.e., what is human about human nature; about the intelligibility of knowing (what philosophers call epistemology); about the intelligibility of a moral or virtuous life (what philosophers call ethics) has provided me with a foundational perspective on the work of educating. The work of educating has traditionally been construed as guiding young people into understanding the world, understanding their own humanity in relationship to participating in the world, and understanding the goodness intrinsic to being human (to human flourishing). So when I talk about the integrity of academic learning, I relate academic learning to the understanding of oneself as participating in the world and understanding how one's participation in the world is tied to the goodness intrinsic to being human.

The Risk of Writing a Book Like This

I was reminded the other day that "privileged groups are more likely to speak and be heard, and in so doing claim the power to name reality" (Kelcourse, 2004, p. 6). As a white, middle class, Anglo-Saxon male, my status as a professor in a prominent research university identifies me as privileged in the sense intended above who tacitly claims the power to name reality. I therefore have to continually remind myself that my perspectives are inescapably limited by my cultural, class, and gendered background, not to mention the limited scope of my scholarly research. What complicates matters even more, I have the temerity to write about ethics—a field of scholarship hotly contested by multiple schools of thought issuing occasional outbursts of rhetorical righteousness in their efforts to establish the superiority of their positions over all others. Worse, still, I am writing about the place of ethics in education, indeed, in the very learning and teaching process—a frightful thought for those purists who fear that ethics in the schoolhouse would directly contaminate the objectivity of the official curriculum and the scientifically based "best practices" of pedagogy (Wiles, 1983). For them, ethics should be limited to the private life, to the subjective beliefs and religious or ideological values that people hold. School learning should deal with facts, not values. The natural and social sciences provide the objective truth about the world and about human nature. Ethics is not scientific. The teaching of ethics is best left to the home and to the religious community. Introducing ethics can only lead to divisive arguments about whose ethics is being taught and embraced. Of course, these arguments that we should not bring ethics into the educating process because it causes disagreements over what kind of ethics to cultivate, ignore the contentious arguments among scholars, parents, teachers, and policy makers over what kind of history to teach in schools, what authors to allow into the school's library and curriculum, indeed, what kind of mathematics, biology, health and world languages should be taught.

Besides, there are no standardized tests to measure student "achievement" in ethics. According to the current orthodoxy, anything that cannot be quantitatively assessed is suspect, or certainly less important. Of course, schools are also supposed to teach patriotism, respect for people of different racial and ethnic backgrounds, sexual orientation, and handicapping conditions, but the only test to measure those learnings is the absence of any documented violations. Likewise, the school is supposed to prevent bullying, sexual harassment, cheating, drug use, and a variety of other inappropriate behaviors. So we have, on the one hand, a fear of introducing ethics into the school, and, on the other, policy mandates to enforce ethical standards prohibiting certain behaviors. To be sure, many of these behaviors are now prohibited by law. If there were no laws against those behaviors, should schools nonetheless prohibit them? Obviously, something's going on here.

Writing a book that advocates the legitimacy, nay, the necessity of "cultivating an ethical school," therefore requires care-full reflection on one's intentions, as well as the assumptions embedded in the text. I candidly admit that my claim of "the power to name reality" rests on all the acknowledged *fallible foundations of legitimacy* upon which most scholarship rests. My scholarly legitimacy—such as it is—rests on the professional practice of teaching in and administering two secondary schools as well as teaching about, studying and writing about education for forty-three years.

At this stage of my life, I think of myself as an educator, talking with fellow educators—all of us doing our best to make sense out of things. I echo what Erik Erikson remarked about his own work: I have "nothing to offer except a way of looking at things" (Kelcourse, 2004, p. 1). Indeed, a "way of looking at things" is what formal and informal education is supposed to communicate. Thus, at the outset of this book I must begin with a necessary disclaimer of offering a final conclusive answer to a very complex educational subject. Every week I uncover three or four additional authors I should read. As I complete the writing of this book I am painfully aware that I did not cover this or that topic or author deeply enough, or at all. Were I to delay writing until I had sufficiently justified everything I say in this book by referencing other authors, this book would never be published. My hope is that my argument is sufficiently grounded in existing scholarship as to earn its right to be considered, as well as to be taken seriously as a reasonable approach to the education of the young.

Overview of the Book

The title of this book is *Cultivating an Ethical School*. It is a substantial rewrite of an earlier book, *Building an Ethical School* (Starratt, 1994). The present book deepens its philosophical base, references more recent scholarship and reflects what I consider an advancement in my thinking. Chapters two and three contain material from the earlier book that has been reworked. Chapter five contains material from a recent publication, *Refocusing School Leadership: Foregrounding Human Development Throughout the Work of the School* (Starratt, 2011). Chapter seven contains material reworked from earlier sources, notably Starratt (2007), and Starratt (2010).

I understand the title of this book as referring both to an ideal school that promotes the practice and understanding of ethical/moral behavior, as well as to a school that can explain the ethical intelligibility that justifies and legitimates the behavior that the school cultivates. Notice that the term "ethical school" indicates that this is an attempt to explain the *ethical good* that is tied specifically to education—that is, to the activity of teaching and learning. It does not mean that such an ethical school will disregard attention to promoting general ethical behavior/choices such as telling the truth, respecting the inviolability of other persons, respecting the property of others, caring for the least of one's brothers or sisters, protecting the rights of others who are suffering injustice at the hands of civil institutions. The book attempts to place the special ethical good of the educational enterprise *within* the practice of what might be termed the general ethics of justice, care, and critique of institutionally unjust arrangements.

The book attempts a meandering logic across ten chapters, set off in two parts. The first part attempts to lay a foundation for educators seeking to cultivate an ethical educating environment. The second part takes up the more specific perspectives on learning and teaching that constitutes the heart of cultivating an ethical school, as well as the surrounding supports for such learning and teaching.

The first chapter places the cultivation of ethical schools against a landscape of the huge challenges facing the human race at the present time. Those challenges require a complex mixture of political, scientific, cultural, technical, philosophical, and ethical responses. The argument is that schools have a part to play in relating the work of learning over the twelve or so years of pre-university schooling to a graduated study of these challenges in their multiform representations. In fact, the argument goes, it would be unethical for educators to carry on the educational enterprise in blissful disregard of these challenges. The academic, social and civic curriculum of the school will provide many opportunities for explicit references to these challenges. Succeeding chapters will allude to some examples of attending to those challenges.

The second chapter elaborates on some of the points in the first chapter, especially to the education of young people in those dispositions and personal qualities that undergird an increasingly mature approach to these challenges. The focus of the chapter unfolds from the basic premise that humans are intrinsically relational and that their human and pre-ethical development involves them in learning to be autonomous, while simultaneously honoring their multiple connectedness to nature, to culture, and to their fellow humans (their family, their friends, and their wider community), and finding the fulfillment of their autonomous and connected life in giving themselves to causes and activities that go beyond self-interest to serving a greater good. Those foundational qualities provide a compass for the mission of the school.

The third chapter of the book expands the horizon from the concentration on the school to the larger field of ethics, what I call general ethics. General ethics pertains to considerations around the daily interactions of everyday life, whether one situates daily life in a family, a neighborhood, a business, a public service enterprise, or a school. One school of ethics deals with the ethics of justice (contractual justice, distributive justice, retributive justice, restorative justice). Another school of ethics deals with the ethics of care (care giving and care receiving in a variety of relationships). A third school of ethics deals with the ethics of critique, which focuses on issues around institutionalized, structural injustice. This chapter argues for a more comprehensive ethic that combines all three schools of ethical scholarship, pointing out how each of the three complements and fills out the other two. This multiperspective ethical framework provides a basis for analyzing and responding to the everyday ethical challenges that arise in schools: bullying, sexual harassment, unfair grading and testing practices, cheating, theft, racial and ethnic prejudice, due process in student or teacher sanctions, etc.

The fourth chapter responds to the question: What do we know about how humans develop into ethical persons? The chapter attempts an overview and critique of some of the more significant scholarship on moral development. One of the key results of this scholarship is to point towards adolescence as the time when many, though by no means all, young people begin to internalize an ethical way of living, connecting it with their growing sense of self-identity.

The fifth chapter attempts to identify ethical development as tied intrinsically to human development, especially as that human development is mapped by Erik Erikson. Erikson sees self-identity as the stage in the life-cycle development as the beginning of a mature ethical way of life. The preceding stages of development attend to those developmental challenges that might be called pre-ethical ways of preparing oneself to become competent to take on the challenges of being ethical. The succeeding stages of intimacy, generativity, and integrity reveal the human as engaging in the full challenges of self-transcendence and human flourishing of the ethical adult. Erikson provides educators with a useful heuristic map for cultivating the development of the pre-ethical and early ethical person within the school agenda, as well as for cultivating that ongoing ethical maturity in the professional staff as they engage the agenda of teaching and learning.

Chapter six opens the second part of the book. Now grounded in a foundational understanding of general ethics and ethical development, we can progress to bringing this grounding into relation with the students' learning agenda and their moral agenda. The chapter suggests a variety of ways to make these connections in the process of cultivating students' ethical development.

Chapter seven takes up the professional ethics of educating, focusing on the ethical good promoted by the work of teaching and learning. The chapter offers a model of the ethics of teaching, focusing on the ethical quality of the teachers' caring relationships with their students, the teachers' own authentic encounter with the world through the curriculum they are teaching, and the teachers' design of learning activities that enable an authentic dialogue between the students and aspects of the world revealed in the curriculum, a dialogue that begins to reveal the students' membership in the world and the world's significance to the students' lives.

Chapter eight steps back from the immediacy of the teaching learning process of the preceding chapters to provide an overview of the elements involved in cultivating an ethical school. By exploring the large and complex agenda of what the work of leading the cultivation of an ethical school involves, the chapter provides educators with a template to employ in assessing a school's present readiness for engaging in the cultivating work in front of them.

Assuming that individual educators reading the book will apply its perspectives to their classrooms rather than to whole school effort, while other educators will be interested in exploring a more ambitious application of the book's perspectives, chapter nine, co-authored with Professor Michael Bezzina, explores multiple ways the book might be applied to various school circumstances. The chapter culminates by presenting an existing effort of several school districts in Australia to cultivate the development of many ethical schools.

The book concludes with a brief chapter that deals with the joys and frustrations of involving oneself in the work of cultivating ethical schools, thereby attempting to relate the more idealistic perspectives of the book to the realities of the work done in schools and its multiple challenges.

I invite you to begin or join the journey this book is taking. The book will be of value to you only if you talk back to it, write notes in the margins to track places of disagreement or applause, talk over some points with colleagues, and especially if you try out some ideas on your own. The book is based on the assumption that learning is a dialogical process in which ideas are taken inside the learner to be tasted and tested out in one's experience, to be related to other, earlier insights and perspectives, and then to be deconstructed and reconstructed as new insights become available.

PART I

Foundations for Cultivating an Ethical School

CHAPTER 1

Cultivating an Ethical School in a Changing Context

The cultivation of an ethical school does not involve superimposing a set of demands on an already overburdened educating work. Rather it involves educators practicing their profession with an integrity that goes right to the core of their work. In other words, the work of educating young people is by its very nature as a profession an ethical work as well as an intellectual work. That does not mean that in practice it cannot degenerate into unethical and irrational or mindless work. However, when one considers the intrinsic good that the work of education intends, it has to do with the inquiry into and contact with the intelligibility of the world as well as the learners' inquiry into a responsible participation in that world thus understood as intelligible. The work conducted in what we recognize as schools inescapably engages educators and their pupils with an academic curriculum, a social curriculum, and a civic curriculum. The work concerns the personal as well as the communal learning of how the world works and of one's actual and potential membership in that world.

Schools introduce young people into the intelligibility of the world of nature through the academic study of the natural sciences and mathematics; to the intelligibility of the social world through the academic curriculum of history and the social sciences; and to the cultural world through the academic curriculum of language arts and the humanities, of literature, music, drama, design, and the visual arts. While the academic treatment of those worlds separates them into differentiated worlds in the abstract, the experience of those worlds by human beings is much more an integrated experience within settings that are simultaneously biophysical, cultural, and social; simultaneously a passive and active process, in which the world is experienced as already there in its particularity and dynamic reality, as well as not there until the person attends to it and by that attention begins to interpret it both perceptually and rationally and emotionally. In school, teachers and learners intentionally set out to explore the intelligibility of the world, and to do that they treat the world as understandable through different clusters of abstractions or "schemas" (Fiske & Taylor, 1991) that compose the academic curriculum. That curriculum parses the world as a biophysical and biochemical world often understood in its mathematical patterns; as a social world of human societies with past and present histories of both rationality and irrationality, and as a cultural world made up of languages, literatures, mores, traditions, life styles, artistic and aesthetic ways of expression, and ideal types of human living. This introduction through the academic curriculum helps to situate learners as *members* of the natural, social, and cultural worlds, both as individuals and as a whole generation of members.

Schools also engage young people in a school's pragmatic social curriculum of learning to live and work with others, including those who differ from them racially, religiously, ethnically, sexually, and ideologically. That learning involves, through the daily mixing with other students, overcoming learned stereotypes that demean or diminish others who are "different." It also involves sharing social spaces (e.g., sitting with different others in the cafeteria); sharing the teacher's attention (e.g., raising one's hand and being called on after others have tried their responses to the teacher's questions); sharing one's ideas in group discussions in classes. It involves learning to be a part of a team whether in sporting events, playing the flute in the school band, or working on the student newspaper. It involves the risky business of making friends, of losing friends, of arguing for one's perspective in a dispute with others.

Schools also introduce youngsters into the initial skills and understandings of civic life, as they learn how to govern themselves within an institution that engages in the larger project of community self-governance with its own institutional agenda of being a school. That introduction means understanding and exercising their rights and responsibilities as citizens of the school community, and of the larger civic community. It means learning the hard lessons of incurring sanctions for violating school rules. It means learning how to manage disagreements with classmates in the schoolyard without getting into name-calling and other inappropriate responses to not getting one's way. It may mean standing up for a classmate who is being bullied by another. It may involve working with classmates under the direction of the teacher at the beginning of the school year to come up with a set of agreements by which the class will govern its conduct.

The learnings of the three curricula—academic, social, and civic—is about learning the meaning, the intelligibility of membership in the world. Membership involves relationships of mutuality, relationships of mutual dependence and mutual rights and responsibilities. As such, those learnings involve both understanding of and being responsible to the implied relationships of the self to the world. In other words, the work of school learning is both intellectual and moral in a very foundational sense.

The Changing Context of Education

The work of educating does not take place in a vacuum. Rather, it is influenced by the social, cultural, and historical world in which the school is embedded, both globally and locally. Even were that context relatively stable, it would influence many, if not most, of the definitions of ethical challenges educators, their pupils, and families face within the educating agenda. The present political and economic, social, and cultural contexts of nations and states around the globe, however, are far from stable. Rather, one can point to major trends on a global scale that are affecting and will continue to impact the process of education and the way ethical concerns may shape that process and be shaped in that process. At least five major trends will affect the education of the young around the globe.[1] The trends identified below will not play out uniformly across every country due to cultural, religious, political, and economic conditions in each locale. Neither will they play out in any simultaneous temporal sequence, again due to various conditions in each country. However, they will all, individually and cumulatively, influence every country's educational process and how ethical issues are defined or ignored in that process. These trends, furthermore, tend to influence one another and thereby feed the sense of urgency in the way governments, intellectuals, cultural leaders, and educators respond to them.

Educators, as most people, do not often step back from the immediacy of their lives, their work, their daily preoccupations with getting through the demands and minor crises of their day, in order to read and reflect upon these large historical trends. Nonetheless, human history does not stand still, especially in this era of instantaneous global communication. The cumulative decisions of individuals, institutions, governments, inventors, explorers, scholars, mothers and fathers, and madmen on a daily basis gradually coalesce into major influences on the patterns of human experience and subsequent human decisions.

Educators are among the most important actors on the world stage, for they prepare (or fail to prepare) the succeeding generations of humans for responsibly engaging the world that is being influenced by these trends. It is not unimportant, then, for educators to attempt to discern the large challenges emerging in the historical moment and to integrate explorations of these challenges into the existing curricula of the school.

Globalization

A major trend that will continue to influence the social and cultural context in which education is carried out is the trend toward globalization. The human world is being reconstructed into a global village, with the networking of nations into regional cooperatives, integrating their economies, their national politics and policies, their laws, their educational systems, their cross border initiatives. The notion of one nation going its independent way without regard for its neighbors is becoming unacceptable. Even in seeking its own national interests and viability, cooperation and collaboration with regional and global partners is increasingly required of all nations (Beck, 2006).

Moreover, in many industrialized nations one sees the rapid increase of immigrants seeking work and a better way of life. For schools in those countries and their municipalities, this has resulted in what some have termed "glocalization" (Mawhinney, 2004), which refers to the ethnic, religious, and racial neighborhoods of recent immigrants who are changing the local, more homogeneous politics of the city or region. The children of these immigrant families arrive at local schools, some with no facility in the national language and others with a comparatively poor educational background. The schools have to make rapid accommodations for them. School policies will vary in the respect or disrespect they ascribe to the culture and language of the new arrivals. In any event, the level of accommodation the schools provide to these students carries clear ethical implications, for these youngsters have both human and civil rights that countries need to respect.

Whether or not physical crossing of borders by immigration continues to accelerate (there are clearly limits to the number of immigrants any one nation can support), the psychological or virtual border crossing through digital technology has already begun on a wide scale. Electronic news media bring almost instantaneous news of natural disasters, outbreaks of virulent diseases, televised sporting events, political uprisings, and political opinions into the homes of millions of viewers around the globe. Introduction to new cultural creations—clothing design and fashion, music, literature, theater, as well as popular culture such as movies and rap music are easily accessible. Points of view concerning human rights, the role of women in society, diverse sexual orientations, religious practices are voiced over global networks. National authorities, even in very closed societies, find it increasingly difficult to prevent or selectively censor ideas and value perspectives flowing through international channels of communication. All of this global communication supports an awareness of both our common humanity as well as the rich diversity of possible expressions of that humanity.

The globalization of information tends to shrink the psychological distance between people of the globe. Schools have to recognize their responsibility to prepare the young to participate as global citizens in responding to the challenges and possibilities presented by widespread global consciousness, global interdependence, and global diversity (Cheng, 2005). In other words, citizens in every country have to surrender their distorted attitudes and beliefs about national sovereignty, cultural superiority, political or economic privilege, historical antagonisms, and stereotypes of enemies and competitors. Instead, they will have to work together simply to survive and sustain some viable future as a global community. Globalization does not destroy national sovereignty; rather, national sovereignty will survive because of globalization (Beck, 2009). Schools have an important role to play in preparing their pupils for membership in a globalized world with all its challenges and opportunities (Cheng, 2005). One might argue that schools fail in their ethical responsibilities if they ignore the globalizing realities of risk that call for a "cosmopolitan vision" (Beck, 2006) of cooperation required by all the nations of the globe and their citizens. This reality of the context of education is connected to the next one.

Environmental Degradation

A second major trend internationally is the concern for environmental sustainability. Responding to the degradation of the environment is every country's responsibility (Mason, 2005). Global resources of energy, arable land, potable water, clean air, species survival and financial capital for investment are shared concerns for every nation's future. Reputable scientists worldwide agree that the planet is rapidly approaching or has already reached the irreversible limit of global warming through carbon emissions into the atmosphere (McKibben, 2010; Stern, 2007). Global warming not only affects rising sea levels due to the melting of the glacial ice cap in various parts of the globe, but causes the gradual drying up of rivers fed by the seasonal melting of those ice caps. In turn, the drying up of rivers leads to the increasing desertification of previously arable land. That, in turn, diminishes the local food resources in those parts of the globe, causing intolerable rises in food prices and potable water.

The gradual exhaustion of oil resources will cause spikes in oil prices that affect every nation's economy. Weather patterns likewise change, bringing more severe hurricanes, storms, and tornadoes. Torrential rains cause mud slides, floods, and increasing displacement of communities and the loss of arable soil. In other words, the planet earth is undergoing severe strains due to the depletion of the resources humans rely on for their very survival. While some countries have begun to respond by mounting various conservation measures, the response so far has been nowhere near what is needed.

Schools cannot solve these environmental sustainability problems, but they have a part to play in helping this younger generation, upon whose shoulders the environmental crisis will fall most heavily in their adult years, begin to understand the depth of the crisis and to explore ways communities and regions and global networks can begin to respond to the crisis (Bowers, 2002; Mumford, 1964). Clearly, these responses will necessarily involve the global community in various forms of cooperation. Schools can help their students link up with students, research centers, and governments in other countries to share common concerns and promising responses. One might easily say that any school's failure to intentionally address the environmental crisis within its academic, social and civic curriculum could be considered a serious moral neglect of their educating responsibilities (Andrzejewski, Boltodano, & Symcox, 2009; Mason, 2005). How that responsibility might be carried out, we hope to address in subsequent chapters of this book.

The International Information Speedway

A third trend that will affect how educators cultivate an ethical school has already been alluded to, namely the rapid emergence of digital technology and its shaping of an international information highway and a knowledge economy, and, more recently, an international form of political activism. First, we can see how this technology assists the globalizing consciousness of students, bringing stories of their peers and their cultures, their challenges, their dreams into the immediate awareness of students who are attending a school, some of whose teachers are ignorant of, or simply inattentive to the drama being played out across the oceans and continents of the world. It is not difficult to perceive an increasing disconnect between students' global awareness and their teachers' relatively circumscribed and parochial attention to their immediate culture and environment. Beyond contact with an international community of peers, local students may be considerably more facile in surfing the web for information and perspectives on topics that interest them, only some of which might connect with one or more academic subjects they might be studying at the time. Nonetheless, by grades six or seven students may have acquired a larger mental encyclopedia of information than some of their teachers who find themselves too busy correcting homework or grading quizzes to surf the web for anything remotely connected to what they are teaching.

Schools and school systems might begin to conduct workshops for teachers on promising digitized programs that could be used to provide differentiated instruction to their students, programs that better reflect advances in the content knowledge of some academic disciplines and its applications to various real life problems, and that might be more culturally responsive to culturally diverse classrooms. Schools or school systems could also provide for their teachers digitized lecture series or professional development units that delve into recent advances in teaching their curriculum (Cheng, 2005).

One may raise the question of the ethical responsibility of all teachers to stay at least as current as their students are on what is available on the internet, both to connect their classes with that material as well as to provide a critique of the value or information bias in that material.

In the not too distant future, school and government officials will wake up to the economies in the schooling effort that can be realized by providing some academic instruction through distance learning programs that can be easily accessed at home or in the local library at a third or less of the cost of a teacher's salary. This could lead to a weekly schedule where students and teachers processed what was being learned at home and in the community via various types of technology and or quasi apprenticeships during two or three days at the school. Obviously, such an arrangement would not be appropriate for the beginning years of schooling that require a more structured and secure environment. Even in the early years, however, such distant or virtual packaging of some instruction accessed at the school site might well serve certain efficiencies in the instructional budget, and might more effectively correspond to the school's ethical responsibility to provide the most effective and up to date instruction that their resources can afford.

To get back to the middle and secondary school years, the opportunities to connect the teaching of academics to real world issues and to student interests and experiences through digital resource is growing by leaps and bounds. This availability of knowledge resources will have enormous potential to diversify the various ways students learn, to provide in-depth research of important issues in both the academic and civic curriculum, through connecting to research resources available on the internet. The resulting teaching–learning process could be enormously enriched, could save the school or school district money, and change the students' engagement in the learning process from a passive to an active frame of mind, with a payoff in student motivation, student intellectual and moral growth, and enhanced student autonomy as a self-activated learner (Cheng, 2005).

One might legitimately ask whether it is more professionally ethical for teachers to hold on to a traditional approach to teaching and learning that is based on a one-size-fits-all textbook, class length, assessment protocol, grading system, and a curriculum that does not represent the way the world really works, instead of teachers engaging with a technology that empowers students to more realistically organize information into meaningful wholes and thereby connect knowledge and understanding to the real world? Obviously, I have created a false dichotomy to construct a rhetorical argument. Nevertheless, between these extremes, where would one take an ethical stance consistent with the professional responsibilities of educators?

The Shift to Relationality

A forth transition involves a deep philosophical shift stimulated, ironically enough, by insights and theories emanating from the natural sciences. It is a shift from a Newtonian view of the basic stuff of all material reality as composed of isolated atoms whose activity causes reactions in other isolated atoms. This atomized view of reality (what Whitehead (1957) argued was "the fallacy of misplaced concreteness") held sway during the emergent European Enlightenment and provided the foundation for viewing individual human beings as likewise isolated from one another and from their natural environment.

Unfortunately, the Newtonian notion of atomic physics carried over to a view of human society proposed by Hume as an artificially constructed community of self-interested persons whose living together was made possible by a "social contract" in which individuals would curb their self-interest from interfering with the "right" of every other person to pursue their self-interest. That view of atomized human beings who collectively made up the human community presented problems for understanding how humans could come to know a world that they stood over against and that stood over against them. The solution to humans' separation from the world would be thought to be solved by science and logical reasoning. Human societies would then be governed by rational principles and laws through the science of politics, economics, and sociology whose findings could then be applied by elected governments who would govern according to the social contract embodied in the constitution or charter of the state.

However, that atomized view of the world has yielded in the Twentieth Century to a view of material reality as a dynamic and fluid field of energy in which every "reality" is related to every other reality simultaneously in space and time. That understanding sustains the view that *the essence of every concrete reality is its relationality to everything else* (Bohn, 1995; Capra, 1982; Lovelock, 1995; Swimme & Berry, 1992; Whitehead, 1957). That view of the nature of reality—of relationality as constituting the essence of all beings—has been applied to understanding human and social reality as well (Zohar & Marshall, 1994).

The argument between the two positions—that of understanding all physical reality as atomized and humans as likewise isolated, self-interested individual beings, as opposed to understanding humans as essentially social and relational (Dewey, 1916)—remains unresolved in North American public life, due to cultural and political divisions (Sullivan, 1982). However, the realities of globalization and the risks facing the global community appear to be underscoring the necessity of recognizing the relationality view of how the world *must* work if the human race is to have a viable future (Habermas, 2006; Ruckriem, 1999).

The Emergence of Reflexive Modernity and Its Pragmatic Epistemology

The past fifty years or so have witnessed the emergence of challenges to early modernity's epistemological claims for the unlimited power of rationality and science and the technologies that science would make possible (Beck, 2009; Habermas, 1971; Horkheimer, 1985; Marcuse, 1966; Ruckriem, 1999). These critical philosophers and social theorists, mostly Europeans, critiqued the Enlightenment's promotion of reason as the highest human faculty whose thoroughgoing exercise would lead to a full emancipation of humans from superstition and oppressive rulers. The Enlightenment had declared that reason and science would situate humans as the *source* of objective knowledge about how the world works. That argument would, in turn, justify human domination over nature, enabling humans to exploit nature's resources for the common good, for national pride and prosperity and also for human profit. Reason and science would enable humans to decide what is normal and what is abnormal, what class in society deserves to rule due to their superior culture and reason, how to control those less desirable elements in society through appropriate sanctions and laws, and, when necessary, through police and military violence (Bradley, 2009; Horsman, 1981, Judis, 2004). Moreover, reason and science would enable the ruling elites to declare what knowledge was legitimate and certain, and what knowledge was unscientific and therefore dangerous or unacceptable, or simply fancifully frivolous.

Despite the public enactment of religious customs among the elites, at least tacitly, science and reason displaced religion for all practical purposes as the tangible means to salvation, with material prosperity flowing from the exploitation of natural resources, guided by science and technical rationality, and, in some cases, taken as evidence of that salvation.

Humans, through the use of reason and science, were thought to be the engines of earthly evolution, replacing natural selection with rational planning and technical rationality. Nature came to be seen as simply there for humans to exploit, much the same as native peoples were simply there, occupying territories that were not being rationally put to good use (Bradley, 2009). European civilization was clearly assumed to be superior to all indigenous peoples due to its advanced science and rationalized form of governance and technology. The "others" would simply have to adapt or disappear (which amounted to the same thing) during a period of colonization (Spring, 2010; Bradley, 2009)

The critique of simplistic understandings of scientific knowledge as providing an objective knowledge of the truth of a relationship among isolated material properties of elements in nature—a truth obtained through an empirical exploration by means of a series of repeated experiments—revealed the distortion of what constitutes scientific knowledge. Under historical scrutiny, scientific knowledge is now seen as more historically limited and fallible. The discoveries of scientific facts by one generation of scientists are challenged by succeeding generations of scientists who see that those facts are only partial explanations and interpretations of the relationships under study; that the results of earlier research were influenced and biased by the instruments and methodologies and theoretical assumptions employed in designing and shaping the experiments which produced the resulting "facts."

While the natural sciences had been viewed as the gold standard for scientific research, the knowledge produced by the social sciences was understood as more fallible, representing statistical probabilities. In the social sciences, moreover, there were greater chances of researcher bias due to gender, cultural, racial, and religious assumptions that affected either the data collection methodologies, sampling procedures, or interpretive theoretical lenses for analyzing and explaining the research data, as well as simplistic statistical procedures for analyzing and reporting the data. Nonetheless, the social sciences embraced the faith in the scientific method and the truth value of statistical probabilities while pursuing with unrelenting vigor a whole range of solutions to human and social problems such as poverty, psychoses, sexual malfunctions, cultural deviance, job satisfaction, the results of various forms of advertising, how elections were won, juvenile delinquency, child rearing practices, organizational engineering, normal marriage and family life, the cataloguing of racial, sexual, and class differences, the structuring of economic systems and economic forecasts. This energy was driven by the expectation that the social sciences could find patterns of personal, social, economic, and political life that would become the norm for a productive and happy, or fulfilled way of living. Just as the natural sciences would show how the world of nature works and thereby provide knowledge of how to control and exploit nature, so the social sciences would provide governments and policy making bodies useful information to normalize and control social and political and economic life. Furthermore, as science provided the foundation for the development of various technologies, industries and disease-controlling drugs, so the social sciences would provide the foundation of technologies and mechanisms for social, economic, and political regulation of social life.

However, the promises of science and technological invention did not automatically usher in a new world of universal contentment. Factory workers, miners, and indentured slaves and farmers found the conditions of work exhausting, with long hours, poor salaries, dependence on the factory, plantation, or mine-controlled housing and store. The technologies and logic of war brought slaughter on the battlefield to unimaginable horror, eventually resulting in the unthinkable annihilation of civilians with the atomic bomb at Hiroshima and Nagasaki. The invention of various gasoline machines and transportation vehicles and coal burning power plants and factories, brought on the beginning of global warming; the invention and widespread use of new chemicals began to infect water supply systems and fisheries. The unregulated use of new medicines had unforeseen side effects on infants and parents. What was supposed to benefit the human condition through modernity's embrace of reason, science, and technology was all too often found to be harmful to both humans and the natural environment.

Ulrich Beck (2009) presents a view of the various risks to humanity's very survival that have flowed from the naïve expectations from science and technological rationality. He does not reject the promise behind modernity's principles—the use of reason, experiment, empirical evidence, logic, seeking human good. He questions, however, the extreme *rationalization* of life, work, economics, politics, national security and national prosperity, national competition with other nations, warfare, policy and legal control, industrialization and production. These extremes have resulted in unforeseen catastrophes that signal a need for a less naïve embrace of what have been taken as the rational logic behind the sciences and technology to the disregard of the human purposes they were meant to serve. Beck argues that the crises facing the nations of the world point to the need for a more reflexive modernity, not the jettisoning of all technology and scientific exploration of the world.

Reflexive modernity is the emerging form of rationality, science and technology within a *necessarily* collaborative effort among the nations of the world to reduce the threats to their very survival—threats such as thermonuclear war and the weapons available to pursue such madness; such as environmental catastrophe; such as the obscene imbalance in material prosperity between rich and poor nations, and between rich and poor citizens within nations; such as the imbalance between access to health services between rich and poor nations (thirty-five thousand children die every day around the globe due to lack of food, potable water, and health care (Wall, 2010)); such as the growing disaffection between younger, unemployed citizens and older, retired citizens whose retirement benefits are jeopardized by faltering economies; such as the still widespread disparities in rights and possibilities between the sexes.

Pedagogical Issues Relating to These Trends

These trends raise serious questions about traditional school pedagogy, and therefore about ethical issues embedded in traditional school pedagogy. We can ask several questions which may begin to surface some of these issues. What is it that teachers are expected to teach? The traditional response would be that teachers are supposed to teach students how to read; how to compute; how to conduct science experiments; how to draw, paint, sculpt, play a musical instrument, read a poem. They are also supposed to teach national and world history, the geography of the earth, the periodic table, the biology of the cell, the physics of electricity, the logic of geometry, the grammar of expository argument, and so forth. Teachers are supposed to teach for understanding of the content knowledge of the academic subject areas, as well as the skills for generating knowledge in those content areas. They are also expected to train students to think like various academic scholars (i.e. to think like mathematicians, like biologists, like historians, like literary critics, like musical critics, like geographers, like environmental scientists). Academic scholars, however, do not learn to think like academic scholars by reading textbooks that tell them what and how to think.

When we look at what teachers are supposed to teach, it would appear that teachers are faced with a subject matter syllabus, a body of knowledge expressed in the syllabus. In the current context of schooling they are expected to teach the content standards of the curriculum as mandated by the state and the local school district. But that knowledge would appear to be a collection of knowledge already finished, already explained in advance in the textbook. It would appear, then, that teachers are supposed to explain this knowledge already explained in the textbook, and that students are then expected to explain the knowledge that has been explained by the teacher and explained in the textbook. Teachers are expected to teach students how to repeat the knowledge that has been assembled by someone else. But students are also expected to construct the knowledge, to interiorize it somehow, to connect it to other pieces of knowledge previously constructed in earlier curriculum units and class lessons. However, that construction has to conform to the correct knowledge already contained in the textbooks and other curriculum materials if one wants to pass the standardized tests that are shaped by national or state curriculum standards.

This kind of pedagogy, then, implies an epistemology, namely, that knowledge is acquired by absorbing and repeating the knowledge contained in books and curriculum materials, not by immediate contact with some reality in the world. Learning is not contact with the world, but contact with an abstract, already systematized and defined knowledge, and frozen in its form in a book. One performs the result of that learning on standardized tests by repeating the knowledge frozen in its book form and definition. Tests do not ask the students to say what the knowledge means to them personally, for tests are not interested in that. The traditional learning process is, as Freire (1970) would have it, a banking process, whereby learners deposit information in their memory vaults to be taken out to buy their way into a successful score on the test. Knowledge thereby loses its transformative power for the learner, since it is literally dead knowledge. What is it students are expected to learn and why should they learn it? In the traditional pedagogy, students are expected to learn the knowledge judged legitimate by the state to conform with its general interpretation of how the world works. This kind of school knowledge tends to be a distortion of how the world actually works. How the world works is far more chaotic, far more unpredictable, far more a struggle among many competing forces, forces of nature, forces of the state, forces of a self-serving economy and a self-serving politic, global stresses and strains, diverse cultural voices, diverse layers of the socioeconomic communities.

Furthermore, this school textbook knowledge, when force-fed in the daily classroom routines, can paralyze the learner since the learner is rarely asked to connect this knowledge to her or his lived knowledge of her or his own personal world. Furthermore, this kind of learning can reinforce the Newtonian atomized view of the universe since the knowledge itself tends to be atomized into pieces of information, strung together with little or no intrinsic relationality to the present and the future, with no significance to the learner's personal, social, or civic life.

If, on the other hand, the teaching of the curriculum were grounded in the ontology of a quantum world of relationality—a relationality to all space and to the past, the present, and the future—then this pedagogy not only positions the learner in relationship to the curriculum as emerging in the past as an historical interpretation of the world then, of how it worked, of its possibilities and challenges, but also how the knowledge of the curriculum positions us for an interpretation of the world now, of how the residue of the past still lingers (for better or worse) in present day social and political and cultural life. Connecting the curriculum to the global unfolding of related issues around how the world works now (or doesn't), of its possibilities and challenges, further enables learners to relate their knowledge to the real world and to their membership in that world (Andrzejewski, Baltodano, & Symcox, 2009).

This kind of pedagogy encourages learners to explore how this knowledge helps them to look into the future, to project the significance of their current learning toward their membership responsibilities and possibilities. A pedagogy that makes this kind of learning possible communicates both an ontology and an epistemology more in harmony with an emerging understanding of world realities and the way knowledge might generate a more dynamic understanding of human membership in the world.

The awareness of membership in the world of the present and the future will be further heightened through the connections to the global realities made possible by the immediacy of digital communications. More than a few commentators are predicting that knowledge itself and the forms it takes are already being unalterably transformed through digital technology (Cheng, 2005; Ruckriem, 1999). It appears that every month new technical "applications" are coming online that make connections to the global and local reality more immediate and practical, that provide an immediate sense of participating in a globally conscious community. That type of increased communication capability augurs the possibility that a more concerted effort to come to agreements on environmental sustainability and social sustainability may begin to surface, and may contribute to more intentional sustainability themes within the curriculum and pedagogy of the school.

Conclusion

At this point we can perhaps understand the argument for cultivating an ethical school that not only stimulates the intellectual exploration of the intelligibility of the world, but also stimulates an ethical exploration of the demands of membership in that world. The argument is that, given the present context of schooling, the continued neglect of the ethical side of the teaching and learning process is no longer an option. The pedagogy and curriculum of the school will *either* express an ontology of possessive individualism (Macpherson, 1962) that separates the individual from the world he seeks to master, as well as an epistemology of knowledge as revealed in a curriculum of already obsolete facts, *or* an ontology of relationality and an epistemology of knowledge gained through a mutual dialogue about intelligibility and significance within a relational, globalized world of both the subject being studied and the learner doing the studying, seen now as learners connected digitally to partners in their local setting as well as in various global settings.

The ensuing chapters will provide examples of how an ethical school can, while drawing out implications of the responsibilities of membership in the worlds of culture, nature, and society, expose students to a variety of perspectives on the large challenges they will be called upon to face. Obviously, not every lesson of every class will be related to these challenges, but the academic, social, and civic curricula of the school can provide multiple and varied opportunities to address some aspect of these challenges so that over the twelve years of their formal schooling the students will grow more aware of the need to bring their values and intelligence to a study of the potential responses available to them.

CHAPTER 2

Foundational Qualities
of an Ethical Person

Introduction

The assumptions behind the last chapter is that schools should prepare young people for membership in a world confronting significant challenges and possibilities, challenges both new and perennial. As Dewey cautioned educators, however, schools should not be about preparing to live, but about living (Dewey, 1916). By that he meant learning by living and living by learning—engaging in age appropriate ways what it means to live in today's world in order to continue to live in tomorrow's world.

The title of this book, *Cultivating an Ethical School,* similarly intends the engagement of young people in living by learning and learning by living in age appropriate ways what it means to live ethically in today's world in order to live ethically in tomorrow's world as responsible members. Schools are about learning, about learning to be and become what we are not fully yet and learning how to get there through patient trial and error. That learning involves going through teacher-designed as well as unplanned learning experiences and reflecting on the lessons learned. That learning involves learning by failures, defeats, mistakes, as well as by successes, victories, and good luck. That learning involves relating to the world and its demands and challenges, learning how to become a human person in the adventures of everyday life with its rewards and disapprovals, learning how to do things, make things, share things. In age appropriate ways they are learning to be and to become the person who will someday graduate from school into a full, mature life.

At the outset of this chapter it is important to state how I conceive the convergence of ethical development with human development. That convergence has its foundation in the ontology of the human. Being ethical addresses the ontological relatedness of our being. We by nature are constituted by our relationality. We live by, with, and through other human beings. We do not constitute ourselves independent of our relationship to others. We are not stand-alone, stand apart, isolated and independent beings who come to birth, indeed, who come to exist at all by our own power. There was a time when we did not exist, and there will be a time when, at least in our embodied state, we will not exist. We did not come into being out of our own nothingness. We came into being as children begotten by parents who belonged to an existing community within an existing society and an existing culture, with physical attributes resulting from the genes of our parents, with a body grown inside another body. We did not make our own bodies and fly in with the stork to arrive at our parents' doorstep. We are constituted by our relationality to all that produced us, physically, socially, culturally, inside of a history that provides the possibilities and limitations of our common adventure into what we call our humanity. That adventure continues to involve struggles and dreams, beauty and terror, heroism and cowardice, triumphs and defeats, inventiveness and stubborn adherence to tradition.

Ethics is what our community and culture and society has come to recognize and name as what violates that relationality as well as honors that relationality. What choices and experiences grow us as fuller, more intentional human beings we call good and desirable; what choices and experiences frustrate or suppress us as fuller, more intentional human beings we call bad or evil, undesirable, dysfunctional, and unworthy of our humanity. Those good or bad choices and experiences either respect and honor our relationality, or disrespect and dishonor our relationality.

One way humans define their relationality is through the term, "membership." We are members of a family, a community, of a tribe or nation, of a cultural and a religious tradition, of an organization and a profession. Enacting one's membership in any one of these groups is the way we enact the relationality of our essential nature, our humanity. Membership confers many "goods" for our lives—friendships, security, work, recreation, language, imagery and rituals for self-expression, and for defending values tied to our relationality. Membership implies and invites participation in the life, values, struggles, and satisfactions of fellow members, by which participation we learn how to overcome an exclusive preoccupation with self, and discover the fulfillment of sharing our lives with others. Our membership also provides us with an identity, with possibilities for contributing something unique from ourselves.

Membership brings to the fore an awareness of rights as well as responsibilities of membership. Rights and responsibilities are two of the faces of relationality for humans. One of the basic responsibilities of membership is to see that the rights of all members are protected and sustained. Furthermore, the exercise of those rights and responsibilities by each individual contributes to the overall welfare of the community one belongs to.

What the preceding argument is getting at is the fundamental point that what societies and cultures consider ethical is very close to or synonymous with what it considers a minimal or virtuous exercise of the relationality that constitutes our lives as human beings. Learning to understand the specifics of our relationality within the worlds of culture, nature, and society, and learning to enact those basic responsibilities and rights of membership in those worlds is what schools promote, or are supposed to promote. Thus, if ethics implies the exercise of our relationality in ways that honor our humanity, the work of schools has to be an intrinsically ethical work in its efforts to promote such understanding and performance.

This chapter takes up what can be considered foundational human qualities of personhood that support living an ethical life. Those qualities will reflect the basic relationality of our humanity, and provide a compass for cultivating an ethical school. In any culture, one might be able to identify these qualities as belonging to persons whom their fellows would consider ethical persons. Persons lacking in these qualities would be less likely to be called ethical, except perhaps in rather superficial ways. A central task of an ethical school is to nurture those foundational human qualities of an ethical life in age appropriate ways. Schools might encourage their students to be law-abiding citizens, by a strict regimen of imposing rules and controlling external rewards and punishments. These efforts might or might not produce law-abiding citizens, but they will not cultivate ethical human beings. This chapter explores what these foundational human qualities are, and how the school might nurture them.

As one moves away from specific actions or choices that might be considered ethical in specific situations and circumstances toward more basic, predispositional ethical qualities, one moves away from ethical disputes about what is the ethical thing to do in this specific instance, toward greater agreement that these general qualities are indeed foundational dispositions for ethical living. These qualities inform all ethical living, although, in any specific instance, the predominance of one quality over the others or the mix of all of them together will differ according to circumstances and perceptions. These basic predispositions to ethical living can provide a broadly acceptable and well-focused foundation for cultivating an ethical education.

The truly ethical person acts as an autonomous agent, acts within the supports and constraints of relationships, and acts in ways that transcend immediate self-interest.[2] In other words, the ethical person has developed relatively mature qualities of *autonomy, connectedness,* and *transcendence.* After exploring these foundational qualities or predispositions of an ethical person, we may draw some general implications for a school that would educate such a person.

In speaking about these qualities, we must first recognize that children and youngsters develop these qualities over time. At any given time in their development, youngsters will exhibit greater or lesser strength in these qualities. Likewise, adults will vary in the strength of these dispositions, depending on whether their development toward maturity has been arrested or supported by significant people and circumstances of their lives. At present, we will explore these qualities as we might find them in a more fully developed adult.

It is also important to acknowledge that the sexes will express these qualities differently. Males are socialized, for better or worse, differently toward autonomy than females. Nonetheless, females will learn to express their autonomy as they develop their human personhood. That expression will not be better than or inferior to the male expression. It will be and should be different in terms of their gendered lives, but as humans, it will be recognized in both as the quality of their autonomy. The same is true about the qualities of connectedness and transcendence. There are normal ways females learn and express their connectedness and transcendence that are different from males. As human beings, however, those qualities will be recognized in both males and females. Although these foundational human qualities will be critical for the ethical development of both boys and girls, the mutual interpenetration of these qualities in the different sexes will be reflected differently at different stages and with different intensities in their development. As teachers move through the various stages of building an ethical school, the men and the women on the faculty will have to discuss these differences and their implications for the design of specific learning activities.

Autonomy

Ethical persons are autonomous. That is, they are independent agents who act out of an intuition of what is right or appropriate in a given situation. Their autonomy is in contrast to those who act out of a mindless routine, or simply because others tell them to act that way, or who act out of a feeling of obligation to or fear of those in authority. Autonomy implies a sense of personal choice, of taking personal responsibility for one's actions, of claiming ownership of one's actions.

Assumed in the notion of autonomy is the sense that the autonomous person is an individual person who has a sense of him or herself as standing out from the crowd. It does not mean necessarily an opposition to all that the crowd stands for. Rather it means a willingness to oppose the crowd in certain circumstances, to walk in a direction different from the crowd if it seems called for. It conveys a certain independence, a definition of one's self that is self-chosen, not imposed by anyone else.

Obviously one does not exist in isolation from communities of meaning and memory. To a great extent, one's identity as a person is formed as a male or female member of a specific cultural community, with its traditions, myths and mores. Yet one becomes an individual by appropriating the community's meanings and mores in a personal and unique way. At times one breaks through the standardized, routinized habits of thinking and acting into new ways of thinking and acting. If one is to overcome the suffocation of the collective, one has to choose one's own meanings. One has, in a sense, continuously to create oneself; otherwise he or she becomes absorbed into the unreflective and undifferentiated ways of thinking and acting of the collective. For humans, it is the painful task of adolescence when one has to begin to separate from parents and from peers to forge one's own identity.

One forges one's own identity especially in creating a world of meaning. One's identity can be shaped by accepting the meanings that the culture conveys. There are customary ways to be feminine or masculine, to be successful, to be popular, to be good or to be bad. By simply doing what the culture (either the peer culture or the parental culture) dictates, one chooses an identity that is hardly differentiated from the generalized identities modeled by the culture. Others will seek to reject what the culture dictates in order to validate their individuality. In adolescence, that often takes the form of distinctive hairstyles, clothing, language and countercultural music, dances, and public heroes. The problem is that many others in one's peer group want to imitate the antiestablishment posture, and so one must go further and adopt an even more unique appearance within the antiestablishment group. Although viewed by adults as unhealthy or crazy, such behavior by adolescents is often a necessary interlude when youngsters can differentiate themselves. Unfortunately, because of involvement with drugs and alcohol, some attempts at self-definition often turn dangerously self-destructive.

However, the process of self-definition, begun early in childhood and a clear focus in adolescence, goes on through young adulthood. After the first extreme efforts at differentiation, the process settles into a less flamboyant, but usually deeper journey. Assuming that one chooses not to conform to socially defined prescriptions, at least in certain defined areas of one's life, how does one justify these choices? Often such choices carry waves of anxiety with them, for they imply that one is cutting oneself off from society's definitions. Staying with what society prescribes offers security and approval. Striking out into the unknown puts one's self at risk. To assume responsibility for one's life, to assert one's autonomy, to create one's meaning where none existed before, one needs to be strong to stand up to such anxiety.

From where does the strength to assume responsibility for one's life come? One source of strength comes from knowledge and understanding, although this knowledge is not necessarily scientific knowledge. Intuition and imagination also lead to knowledge and understanding. The strength comes from knowing that there are options, of knowing at least some of the options quite well. It also comes from knowing oneself well enough to know why one is afraid to define one's own meaning. Those who live amidst grinding poverty and little hope, however, cannot easily see options and believe that they are already defined by outside forces.

Becker, citing Adler and Fromm, asserts that "neurosis is a problem of the authority over one's life" (1968, p. 258). If one is afraid to move forward under one's own power, which is what it means to be autonomous, it is because that power has been turned over to someone or something else. In that case, one finds the source of power that sustains one's life externally to him or herself. The most common external source is the transference relationship in which one gets personal power from the father figure, from someone in authority. A second major source of power is from a supernatural, personal god, or some transcendent nature or world soul. A third source of power is in the cultural game itself, the everyday rituals and performances that are already in place and thoroughly scripted. Insofar as one turns over one's independence to any of these external sources of power, one loses autonomy.

The strength to be free comes not simply from knowledge, even the therapeutic knowledge of our former bondage to an external source of power. The strength to be oneself can only be fully gained in relationships to other human beings. In authentic relationships, others give us the courage to be ourselves. Here we have the paradox of autonomy. One cannot be autonomous in isolation. Striving to be totally oneself by oneself reveals one's incompleteness, one's poverty, one's existential loneliness. One makes contact with "reality," with the rich world of meaning, by reaching out beyond the isolated self. As Martin Buber put it:

Human life touches on absoluteness in virtue of its dialogical character, for in spite of his uniqueness man can never find, when he plunges to the depth of his life, a being that is whole in itself and as such touches on the absolute. Man can become whole not in virtue of a relation to himself but only in virtue of a relation to another self. This other self may be just as limited and conditioned as he is; in being together the unlimited and the unconditioned is experienced. (Buber, 1955, pp. 167–168)

Our knowledge and our meanings and our uniqueness are validated in interpersonal relations. Our autonomous decisions reflect both our independent judgments and a choice to act in relation to others. Aggressive and adversarial competition, then, is not natural; when it leads to selfish isolationism, it is in fact destructive of both the individual and the community. Buber (1955) offers a way out of the either/or conundrum of narrow individualism or constricting collectivism by showing that the depth of reality is essentially relational. He offers us a vision of society working toward a transcending ideal, but an ideal rooted in autonomous individuals who find their fulfillment in living relationships.

Dewey (1927) also speaks of society working toward this transcending ideal, an ideal in which human beings, working together, each with a reservoir of talent and intelligence, continuously recreate their society in progressive transformations, and in the process find their own individual fulfillment. He called this the ideal of democracy. In reality, Dewey acknowledged, democracy always falls short of the ideal, but continues to work toward that ideal. The human condition is defined both by the failure and the successes of that effort.

The ethical person must be autonomous. Only in one's autonomy can one bring one's unique personal gifts to an ethical exchange. Only autonomous actors can claim responsibility for their choices. Only autonomous agents add a piece of their own lives, a quality of their unique selves to the ethical act. What constitutes the act as *ethical* is, as a matter of fact, that it is the intentional act of *this person,* not the act of an unreflecting, robot-like human who is following a routine prescribed by someone else, or is driven by irrational urges. Hence, we can see that one of the primary human tasks facing a young person is to become autonomous, to claim his or her own life. One can speak, then, of a deep moral obligation to become autonomous, for only then can one claim membership in a community of moral agents. It follows that the formation of autonomous persons is a primary ethical task of schooling.

Connectedness

The ethical person is connected (Scheler, 1957). As we saw above, the autonomous person cannot authentically express her or his autonomy except in relationships. Every relationship is distinct. It offers unique possibilities because of the qualities that each person brings to the relationship. It is also bounded by the limitations that each person brings to the exchange. What one might expect from one person might be unfair to expect from another. A woman brings certain qualities to a relationship; a man brings other qualities. An older person might be expected to be more flexible in a relationship than a younger person; relationships involving people from the same culture are often different than those involving people from different cultures (Hallowell, 1999).

Circumstances set limits as well as create opportunities in relationships. Work related relationships hold opportunities for creative teamwork in technical areas; neighborhood relationships offer opportunities for more family oriented or recreational activities. Customer or client relationships are different than employer–employee relationships.

Hence it is clear that ethical behavior, while always involving interpersonal relationships, is shaped by the circumstances and status of the persons involved. Acting ethically requires one to be sensitive and responsive to the other person *within* the circumstances and the context.

Within this theme of connectedness, we cannot avoid discussing relationships between the sexes. Here it is so important to be sensitive to the revolution going on in the redefinition of what constitutes masculinity and femininity. Since this revolution is still in its beginning stages, it would be premature to attempt to redefine an education that 'correctly' socializes young people into the possibilities and responsibilities involved in male–female relationships. Yet some attempt must be made, starting from the recognition that traditional definitions of male and female are distorting of the possibilities for both males and females, in their separate lives and for their lives in relationships with one another. No longer can education about the human be dominated by male categories and male frameworks.

The school agenda for both males and females requires the simultaneous attention to equity and to difference. Attention to equity requires that girls and boys have equal access to and encouragement in all programs in the schools. Attention to difference requires that girls and boys have opportunities for same-sex activities and for same-sex discussions of the social expectations of each sex role. It also requires appropriate cross-sex discussions of their differences and the issues and problems that flow from these differences. A variety of authors provide perspectives on either female or male developmental issues (Belenky, Clinchy, Goldberg, & Tarule, 1986;

Gilligan, 1982; Hollway, 2006; Johnson, 1983, Jordan et al. 1991; Pearson, 1986; Sichtermann, 1986).

Attention to gender, circumstances, and context, however, calls our attention to the cultural scaffolding of all relationships. One does not act with another person according to a uniform, universal script. Rather, humans express themselves in relationships according to an infinite number of cultural artifacts and cultural signs (Chatwin 1987; Goffman, 1959; Green, 1985; Shils, 1981). The clothing one wears at various occasions, the language employed, the formality or informality one adopts—all these are culturally prescribed. Hence, acting ethically in any situation requires a knowledge of and respect for the culture one inhabits. Acting ethically means being sensitively connected to the values expressed by the sign and symbol system of that culture, for they make up the foreground and the background of relationships as they unfold. So it is not simply a question of one person in relation to another person; the relationship is supported as well as limited by the culture in which the two parties live their lives.

Every culture is a rich endowment, an enormous inheritance. It contains and expresses the history of a whole people over the course of many centuries: their struggles, their triumphs, their tragedies, their sense of heroism, their sense of failure, their ideals and their values. One acts ethically within that culture, within its possibilities and within its limits. No culture is perfect, no culture has finished its human journey. Hence the ethical person knows that the inheritance is also a burden. It has standards to be lived up to; it has standards to be surpassed; it has a bias against other cultures; it has a history of shameful behaviors as well as honorable behaviors; it has frontiers to be reached and perhaps expanded. Ethical persons, experiencing connectedness to their culture and to other persons, know that the culture sustains their lives, and that they have a responsibility to sustain the life of the culture. Sustaining that life happens in one's relationships and involves a kind of loyalty. Though the awareness is normally tacit, ethical persons approach one another as cultural beings, and yet because of the culture they share, they can approach each other in a discovery of uniqueness, where the humanity of the other person is discovered beyond, so to speak, cultural symbols, or as fresh embodiments of those symbols.

This adds, of course to the paradox of autonomy. One is autonomous, yet one's autonomy is as a cultural being. As one supported by that cultural life, one bears responsibilities to it, to uphold its honor, its ideals, and to pass on the best of that culture to the next generation. The autonomous cultural agent, however, is different from the unreflective cultural agent who is a slave to the culture, who cannot distinguish the shortcomings of the culture—for example, in the way it treats women, or peoples of certain other cultures. The autonomous cultural agent can be a critic of his or her culture and see that as an act of responsibility to the culture. For beyond culture, there is humanity, to which all cultures bear responsibility.

Ethical beings are also connected to their natural environment. That environment provides air to breathe, food to nourish, the raw materials for food and housing, transportation and industrial production. This connection to nature in the present has a long past as well. Every person contains in his or her genes, so to speak, the history of evolution and the effects of cosmic time. As beings embedded in nature, yet having enormous power to affect nature, we have responsibilities to preserve the natural world itself, not simply to ensure the survival of the human species (Macy, 1990). Unbounded human exploitation of nature seemed a human right not very long ago. Now we recognize that we have to be far more respectful of natural processes of a nature that is endangered. Our connectedness to the earth is now seen as bringing ethical obligations to preserve the earth (Augros & Stanciu, 1987; Bateson, 1979b; Macy, 1990; McKibben, 2010). Our connectedness to the race, in both evolutionary time and in the future, brings responsibilities both to our forebears and to our progeny.

We cannot leave this quality of connectedness without speaking of its political and social implications. In the United States, we happen to live in a democracy, which we are coming to realize is a fragile collage of many voices, many distinct communities. One view of democracy is that it is a society made up of separate individuals, each pursuing his or her own self-interest, joined together in a social contract which protects the rights of all individuals to pursue self-interest as long as it does not infringe on the rights of others. The problem with this view is that it ignores the real bonds that make life in the community morally compelling (Bellah et al., 1985).

Another view of democracy sees humans as inherently social, whose individual moral good is achieved and sustained only in community, through the bonds of blood to be sure, but also through the bonds of neighborliness, interdependence, and brotherly and sisterly affection. In this view, our humanity reaches its highest moral fulfillment in community. Without the relationships of community, which constitute not just necessary interdependencies, but also an intrinsic good, life would not be worth living. This is not to say that these relationships do not involve conflict, disloyalty, disagreement. But these relationships—even in conflict and struggle—define the context of human moral striving, the effort to agree on what constitutes our common good. Democratic political and social life does not guarantee a continuous experience of freedom, equality and brother/sisterhood; rather, those are the goals and purposes continually pursued in democratic give-and-take in public life. It is in being connected to that community with those very ideals, and the procedural rights and responsibilities that govern their pursuit, where we discover our truest moral selves (Sullivan, 1982).

In discussing 'conscience as membership', Green (1985) makes a point of fundamental educational importance to the formation of a sense of connectedness. He speaks of the necessity of empathy. In any discussion of what the group or social collective should do, there will be differences of opinion. In order for a moral choice to emerge (not simply an arithmetical calculation of allowing the consequences of X's opinion and Y's opinion to be figured into the decision, nor a calculation of political favor-swapping) one has to engage seriously the perspective of others. This means entering into an empathetic appreciation of the value and legitimacy of those perspectives, a kind of taking those perspectives as if they were one's own in order to understand the reasoning and to feel the affective colorations embedded within them. For our purposes, this insight into the psychological and existential dynamic of empathy enables us to see how one gains a sense of connectedness. It is by entertaining the legitimacy of the claims and perspectives of others, by imaginatively taking the reality of the other inside ourselves and seeing how it feels to be that other in these circumstances. This applies to the experience of being connected to family and ethnic roots, to friends, to the environment, and to the civic community. This dynamic of empathy provides one clue to developing the quality of connectedness in an educational setting, a dynamic that involves both understanding and feeling, a kind of sympathetic knowing (Starratt, 1969).

Green, however, roots his foundation for moral education in the formation of a conscience of *membership*. If there is to be a strong sense of a public, a sense of a shared life together, a sense of concern for the common good, then citizens must learn to be bound by a strong sense of membership. Membership brings certain rights, but it also brings responsibilities. As was mentioned above, there is a strong sense of individualism within American culture. Often that sense ignores the notion of an "us;" it is more about *my* rights. Green rightfully insists that in our moral education, we continually position ethical obligations as connected both to individuals and to the group. If it were a good thing for John Doe to do such and such, would it not be a good thing for *us* in similar circumstances to do also? If something pertains to membership, ought it not to pertain to *our* membership? This issue will arise in later chapters concerning one's sense of moral identity, as well as concerning the moral character of learning.

Transcendence

Transcendence is a term that might frighten some people off. For some it signifies an attempt to climb above our humanity, to leave it behind in a journey toward some higher, more spiritual form of life. This seems to be the Platonic ideal, where the philosopher ascends through a process of spiritual purification and mental abstraction to grasp the eternal form, The Good. I am not using the term in this sense. Rather, it has for me three levels of meaning, one dealing with the reach for excellence, the other with the turning of one's life toward something or someone else, and the third with achieving something heroic.

On the first level, transcendence means going beyond the ordinary, beyond what is considered average. In this sense, it means striving for and achieving a level of excellence that exceeds anything one has ever done before. The standard of excellence will be relative both to the type of activity involved (playing the violin, or high jumping, or writing poetry) as well as the person involved (a physically uncoordinated person, a mature professional athlete, a sight-challenged person). Transcendence on this level means a struggle to stretch the limits placed upon us by nature, to create a purer sound, to leap against gravity's pull, to see clear through to the essence of a feeling and capture it just so in the perfect metaphor. It is the struggle for the perfection of a human talent, and it is a struggle precisely because the possibilities of reaching that perfection, let alone of sustaining it, are limited by self-doubt and our very ordinariness as human beings (Nussbaum, 1990).

On another level, transcendence means going beyond self-absorption (which the search for excellence can sometimes promote) to engaging our lives with other people, whether to share their life journey with them, or to work with them towards some goal that benefits a group or society in some way or other. Transcendence in this sense also means going beyond the ordinary. By the very ordinary nature of our social existence, we have to make room for others in our lives. People often intrude at times when we wish they wouldn't, but we respond to them with polite tact, and go back to our project as soon as their intrusion is over. We learn to accommodate others, sometimes cheerfully, sometimes reluctantly. This is what minimal or ordinary social relations require. Transcending this level of social relations means taking on the burdens of others, caring for them, putting ourselves in their place—not once a month, but very often, if not habitually. It means anticipating their needs, surprising them with thoughtful gifts. It means finding our fulfillment in easing the burdens of others, making them laugh, helping them finish a project. This form of transcendence is clearly a foundation for the exercise of the ethic of care.

It also means being able to invest one's energies in a collective activity with others that serves some valued purpose beyond self-interest. That form of transcendence involves becoming a part of something larger than one's own life. Through that involvement one moves beyond an exclusive concern for one's own survival and necessities of life to an effort to serve a larger common good. That common good invests the actions of the individual with higher value, with higher moral quality.

As involvement with others becomes more total, it moves toward the third level of transcendence, which is what I call the heroic. One can invest one's energies in other people and in a cause—up to a point. At some point, people say to themselves, "OK that's enough for now. Now it's time for my life, my interests, my leisure and recreation." The more total involvement is the willingness to sacrifice some of what most people would say were one's legitimate rights to "time off," "time for oneself." Teachers who consistently stay late and arrive early in order to help out youngsters having difficulty with their school work, or just plain difficulty with life; social workers who consistently go the extra mile for their clients in getting them needed assistance; doctors who continue to spend quality time with their patients, listening to their anxieties; public officials who treat ordinary citizens with as much respect and courtesy as they do the "important people"; store managers who spend countless hours devising ways to improve staff morale and customer service—these are people who transcend the ordinary and embrace heroic ideals of making a difference in people's lives. The recognition of some of the great heroes, like Mother Theresa or Vaclav Havel, with public awards like the Noble Prize does not belittle the significance of the more everyday expressions of heroism.

Heroism, like transcendence, is often misunderstood. Heroes, it is thought, are those rare exceptions to the rule of self-interest, to the norm of mediocrity. While it is true that heroes are outnumbered by the less-than-heroic, the desire for heroism is a common human trait. From our early childhood years onward, we ask, "What is the value of my life?" We demand to be recognized, as Ernest Becker (1971, p. 76) points out, "as an object of primary value in the universe. Nothing less." Becker recognizes this as a desire to be, in one way or another, a heroic contributor to the human journey, and that nothing less will satisfy us.

Our interpretation of what constitutes heroic action is, of course, mediated by our culture and subcultures through the symbolic values it attaches to some achievements. An Olympic gold medal, a scholarship to Oxford University, an Oscar-winning performance are all culturally significant, heroic activities. On a smaller stage, the neighborhood dominoes champion walks around his turf with heroic stride, for, in that ambiance, he is somebody to be reckoned with.

By claiming transcendence as a basic human quality we recognize that it is foundational to human moral striving. If this quality is not developed during youth and young adulthood, then a mature ethical life is simply not possible. Again, Green (1985) is helpful here in pointing to an educational source for nurturing this sense of transcendence, namely the great writers of imaginative literature. In conversations with these poets of the heroic, these prophets and utopians, youngsters are exposed to the images of possibilities for human life. By exposure to stories of great human striving, their own heroic aspirations are kindled; these exemplars provide models for possible imitation. Biographies of great leaders in history bring reality perspectives to frame the more utopian idealism of imagination. The point Green makes is important, however: our transcendent aspirations are nurtured in and through the heroic imagination.

When transcendence is joined with the qualities of autonomy and connectedness, we begin to see how the three qualities complement and feed each other in the building of a rich and integral human life. Being autonomous only makes sense when one's autonomy can be in relation to other autonomous persons, when the uniqueness and wealth of each person can be mutually appreciated and celebrated. Connectedness means that one is connected to someone or something different from oneself. Hence it requires an empathetic embrace of what is different for the autonomous actor to make and sustain the connection. Community enables the autonomous individual to belong to something larger; it gives the individual roots in both the past and the present. However the community is not automatically self-sustaining, but is sustained by autonomous individuals who transcend self-interest in order to promote the common good, who join with other individuals to recreate the community by offering satisfying and mutually fulfilling services for one another, services of protection and support, care and help, joint action on a common project, celebration of a common heritage, honoring a community tradition by connecting one's own story to the larger story of the community. This give-and-take of life in the community simultaneously depends on and feeds the heroic imagination of individuals whose action, in turn, gives new life to the community.

Although we speak of these three foundational qualities of an ethical person in a somewhat abstract way, we don't want to think of them as a list of virtues that we set out to acquire. We are speaking of an ethical *person* who has a unity and integrity, whose actions reveal qualities that shine out as from a diamond. These qualities of an ethical person, however, do not fall from the sky. They are developed in action, through choices that are acted upon. These qualities are never achieved as an acquisition. They are always to be found in the action of specific persons in this moment, in these circumstances, with these people, and hence never perfectly or fully expressed. They are achieved only in the doing and in the doing-constantly-repeated (Meilaender, 1984).

What I have described above is more like an ideal type of person. This person rarely if ever exists in perfect form. Most of the time human beings reflect imperfect efforts in the direction of truly autonomous, connected and transcending actions. The ideal type, however, serves a purpose. It points to an ideal we try to reach. It also provides a guide for those who would educate toward ethical living. By providing opportunities for youngsters to exercise autonomy, connectedness, and transcendence, educators enable youngsters to experience the fulfillment and satisfaction of the way of being human. They learn the lesson that living ethically is the fulfillment of their human nature.

If these qualities are foundational in a developing ethical person, then an ethical school will be concerned to nurture those qualities and discourage the development of their opposite qualities. Hence, teachers need to reflect on how they can use the everyday activities of youngsters in their classroom and other areas around the school to nurture these qualities. Of course, youngsters develop in recognizable patterns, so that what might be appropriate for a ten-year-old may not be appropriate for a sixteen-year-old. How one nurtures the sense of transcendence in kindergarten would differ from an approach taken in seventh grade. The three qualities can be supported in every grade, however, in ways that are suitable for the children, but it would be a mistake to expect all the children to manifest these qualities in the same way. Sex, race, culture, and class will all nuance the child's expression of autonomy, connectedness, and transcendence. Class-bound and ethnocentric teachers will have difficulty with such varied expressions. The sensitive teacher will observe the different expressions and listen to youngsters explain their behavior. Over time such teachers will be able to promote these qualities within an appropriate range of plurality and diversity.

This chapter has explored the human qualities that form a foundation for ethical maturity. Recognizing that young people in school are in those formative years before adulthood, before they will be held accountable by the community to act ethically, we can see how the nurturing of these qualities in young people begin to prepare them for the responsibilities of adulthood. Teachers should be expected to model these qualities in their professional practice. The academic, social and civic curriculum of the school should engage the development of these qualities. Moreover, the school as public institution should exhibit adult ethical standards. These standards would be considered as general ethical standards expected of adults in their everyday lives. In the next chapter we will look at some of the schools of thought that deal with what might be considered general ethics, the ethics of adult daily living. The cultivation of an ethical school involves the adults in the school in teaching these general ethical principles by example. As we will see in the next chapter, there are some disputes among scholars of ethics about what constitutes the core or essential ethical concerns of general ethics. Educators attempting to cultivate an ethical school should come to some agreements about how to frame ethical questions so as to deal with ethical issues that arise in the daily practice of conducting schools.

CHAPTER 3

A Multidimensional Ethical Framework

This chapter presents a multidimensional view of ethics that can guide the decisions, policies, and activities of educators and the learners as they engage the school's threefold curricula of academics, personal growth, and citizenship.[3] The chapter carries the burden of being theoretical enough to provide a grounding in ethical theory for the community of educators whose academic background in ethics may be rather thin, and yet is sufficiently focused on the educating context to connect the theory to their practice. What is presented here, therefore, is not ethical theory for ethical theorists (though it is sufficiently theoretical to reflect a grounding in mainstream scholarship), but an ethical theory for educational practitioners. This will provide a large framework for subsequent chapters to delve into its application to the educational enterprise.

In the field of ethics one can find a variety of frameworks that provide a rationale for a form of ethical education. Some frameworks would stress an ethic of justice as an overall framework; others would stress an ethic of care; still others would criticize those ethics as politically and culturally naïve, preferring an ethic of critique that addresses the many actual social injustices to be found in contemporary societies around the world. I want to suggest that we consider a large framework that embraces all three schools of thought in a multidimensional framework. I believe that each of these schools of thought provides direction for an important part of an ethical education, but that no one of them taken alone is sufficient. Furthermore, I believe they reflect the dynamic involved deep in the psychological, physical, and ontological structures of human beings as they attempt to enact what constitutes their very humanity, the way they are nature becoming human, the way they consciously and subconsciously enact their humanity, and they way they enact their very being as humans.

Each ethical perspective will be developed consecutively. While attempting to remain faithful to the theory, or body of theory from which the theme was selected, the exposition will be related to the ethical implications of the educating context. Underneath these three ethics, of course, are the irreducible assumptions about what is valuable in human life in which every theory is grounded. A full discussion of the ontology and epistemology and psychology behind these constructs, however, would paralyze, I fear, the very attempt to develop these thematic building blocks. One hopes, however, that the chapter might provide sufficient connections to the scholarship and the reasoning behind this development of a multi-dimensional view of ethics that in turn, might provide educators a firm footing for integrating these ethical perspectives into their thinking and practice of their profession.

The Ethic of Care

The ethic of care focuses on the demands of relationships, not from a contractual or legalistic standpoint, but from a standpoint of regard for the very "givenness" of the other, whether that other is another person, a Vivaldi concerto, or a first summer rose. This ethic places human persons in relationships of absolute value; each other enjoys an intrinsic dignity and worth, and, given the chance, will reveal genuinely loveable qualities. Thus, an ethic of caring requires fidelity to persons, a willingness to acknowledge their right to be who they are, an openness to encountering them in their authentic individuality, a loyalty and responsibility to the relationship, even at a distance (Hollway, 2006). Such an ethic does not demand relationships of intimacy (though it may include such relationships); rather, it postulates a level of caring that honors the dignity and integrity of each person and desires to see that person enjoy a fully human life. Furthermore, it recognizes that it is in the relationship that the specifically human is grounded; isolated individuals functioning only for themselves are but half persons; one becomes whole when one is in relationship with another, and with many others.

I place the ethic of care first, because it is primary. Care is so fundamental, that without it humans would cease to be human. Humans can live with injustice; they can survive in structurally unjust conditions. But without being cared for, without being connected to significant others in mutual expressions of caring, the prospects for existing as what we recognize as human beings seem impossible. Not only do infants who are abandoned by their parents suffer irreparable damage to their chances for a fully human life, but children raised by parents who abuse them, continually humiliate them, show almost total disregard for them—these children also suffer a loss of their sense of worth as a human being. What gives them a chance to recover a more human existence is a relationship with a caring person and a succession of caring persons. Adults who have enjoyed a loving family life, who have acquired a good sense of themselves, can nonetheless lose faith in themselves when placed in settings where they have no friends, where they are surrounded by people who are habitually nasty, aggressive, uncaring. Without friends, without people who care for us, we find ourselves adrift, emptied out, threatened. Loneliness is not an uncommon, if passing, human experience. But never-ending loneliness leads to suicide in one form or another (Becker, 1971; Fuller, 2004; Riesman, 1950).

Humans are social beings who need to be validated in caring relationships. More than being fairly treated, they need someone to love them, and someone, in return, to love. We hear some claiming that respect is the basic virtue. However much I am respected, nonetheless, if I am not loved and cherished by someone, the respect I receive from others will not be enough to feel fulfilled in life. Likewise, if I have no one to care about and for, my life is likewise truncated, diminished. Caring is an intrinsic law of life for humans. Where it is plentiful, humans flourish. Where it is thin and artificial, humans grow spiritually thin and humanly artificial. Caring is an ethic in the bones of humans. They know, intuitively if tacitly, that they are obliged to care for one another if they are to be human. We come to be a human being through being cared into existence and cared into growing, and cared into finding oneself through caring (Becker, 1971; Bellah et al., 1985; Buber, 1958; Fromm, 1956; Hallowell, 1999).

In 1982 Carol Gilligan published a groundbreaking book, *In a Different Voice*, in which she reported on research that revealed that women's socialization and therefore their psychological development differed from that of men. Whereas the research by Lawrence Kohlberg (1981) suggested a cognitive moral developmental process that moved toward successively more mature judgments about the morality of justice, Gilligan's research on young women suggested that their moral development was much more centered on an ethic of care and responsibility to other persons. Whereas an ethic of justice tends to deal with the rights that accrue to human beings within communities and societies, and tends to emphasize the separateness of human beings in their individuality and therefore their rights *in opposition* to the community's ownership of the individual, an ethic of care tends to deal with the relationality that binds humans together, and the attendant responsibility of responding to the other's needs as another human person.

The ethic of care is not limited to interpersonal relationships such as might be found in families, in friendships, in marriage partners. The ethic of care also reaches beyond these relationships to caring for other persons in need, whether they be sick and infirm, impoverished, unjustly persecuted or oppressed (Hollway, 2006; Skeggs, 1997). It also extends to fellow workers on the job, and to fellow citizens one encounters in everyday life. Caring is the ethic that binds communities together in sociality. Justice is the ethic that binds people together in the demands that accrue in virtue of their rights as citizens and as individual human beings. Within the ethic of care, I am not responsible for other people in view of their rights, but in view of sharing with them a common humanity, a humanity endowed with beauty, talent, and promise, but also a humanity that is fragile, continually wounded by its ambivalence, and needing care. That common humanity that all humans share with one another is a given; it is not legislated by the state; nor is it earned through heroic effort or extraordinary talent. It is something that is given by being born a human being. The ethic of care is also a responsibility that is given by being born a human being.

A school community committed to an ethic of caring will be grounded in the belief that the integrity of human relationships should be held sacred, and that the school as an organization should hold the good of human beings within it as sacred. This ethic reaches beyond concerns with efficiency, which can easily lead to using human beings as merely the means to some larger purpose of productivity, such as an increase in the district's average scores on standardized test, or the lowering of per-pupil costs.

A school committed to an ethic of caring will attend to the 'underside' of the diverse interactions among members of the community, that is, to those motives that sometimes intrude, even slightly, in an exchange with a teacher, student or parent. Sometimes those motives involve the desire to dominate, to intimidate, to control. Sometimes those motives involve racial, sexual, ethnic and age stereotypes that block the possibility of honest communication. Sometimes a teacher feels insecure in the face of strong and assertive students and feels the need to put them in their place. Sometimes an administrator is not even aware of the power she or he has in the eyes of teachers and recklessly toys with the teacher's insecurity by some lighthearted ridicule of a classroom activity.

When these underside issues dominate an exchange, they block any possibility of open and trusting communication. Mistrust, manipulation, aggressive and controlling actions or language on the part of an administrator, teacher, or student can lead to relationships that are hypocritical, dishonest, disloyal, and dehumanizing. People who are fairly secure in their sense of themselves and in their professional role are not overly affected by these underside motives; few, however, are entirely free from them in every circumstance. If these motives are understood and acknowledged initially, they will not distort the exchange in excessively manipulative or negative ways. An exchange between a teacher and student can move beyond a superficial ritual to a contractual obligation to a relationship of caring, when there is a deep attention to the unique human beings involved in the exchange, to issues of self-esteem, personal confidence and ego anxieties.

Besides developing sensitivity to the dignity and uniqueness of each person in the school, educators promote an ethic of caring by attending to the cultural tone of the school. Often the use of language in official communiqués will tell the story. Formal abstract language is the language of bureaucracy, of distance. Humor, familiar imagery and metaphor, personalized messages are the language of caring. Through reward procedures and ceremonies as well as school emblems, school mottos, school songs and other symbols, the school communicates what it cares about. When the school rewards academic competition in ways that pit students against each other, when the awards are few and go only to the "top students" in the formal academic disciplines, then the school makes a clear statement of what it values. Other ceremonies and awards that stress caring, cooperation, service, and teamwork, send different messages. Some schools clearly promote a feeling of family and celebrate friendship, loyalty and service. Laughter in the halls, frequent greetings of each other by name, symbols of congratulations for successful projects, frequent displays of student work, hallways containing pictures of groups of youngsters engaged in school activities, cartoons poking fun at teachers and administrators—these are all signs of a school environment that values people for who they are. When youngsters engage every day in such a school community, they learn the lessons of caring, of respect, of service to each other. With some help from peers and teachers, they also learn how to forgive, to mend a bruised relationship, to accept criticism, to debate different points of view (Noddings, 1992; Christensen, 2009).

The Ethic of Justice

While one can assent to the priority of the ethic of caring within an educational setting, it remains an incomplete answer to the complexities of running a school. The school is also an organization that requires procedures, policies, and structures that will provide to the work of teaching and learning a necessary order and predictability, a sense of purpose and accountability toward the work. A school has to have some way of governing its internal life. An ethic of justice provides some explicit response to the issue of self-governance. We govern ourselves by observing justice. That is to say, we treat each other according to some standard of justice that is uniformly applied to all our relationships. The theory of justice we employ to ground those standards itself requires a grounding in an anthropology and epistemology. Plato explored this grounding in *The Republic*; his search was to be pursued by a long line of philosophers up to the present day.

Currently there are two general schools of thought concerning the ethic of justice. One school can trace its roots to Thomas Hobbes in the seventeenth century, and can find a contemporary expression in the work of John Rawls (1971). In this school of thought, the primary human reality is the individual, independent of social relationships; the individual is conceived as logically prior to society. Individuals are driven by their passions and interest, especially by fear of harm and desire for comfort. Individuals enter into social relations to advance their own advantage. Individual will and preference are the primary sources of value. Therefore social relationships are essentially artificial and governed by self-interest. The maintenance of social life requires a social contract in which individuals agree to surrender some of their freedom in return for the state's protection from the otherwise unbridled self-seeking of others. In this school of thought, human reason is the instrument by which the individual can analyze in a more or less scientific fashion what is to his or her advantage, and to calculate the obligations to social justice called for by the social contract. As Sullivan (1982) comments, in its more benign application, this theory conceives of social justice as a social engineering to harmonize needs and wants of self-serving individuals in society.

Lawrence Kohlberg carried on this tradition of moral theory, only he claimed to go beyond the traditional standoff between "is" and "ought" found in Hume and Kant. In his research Kohlberg claimed to have documented an isomorphism between psychological development of moral reasoning and normative ethical theory. His research indicated that as humans moved from one moral stage to a higher moral stage, they moved toward formal moral criteria of prescriptiveness and universality. Their higher moral reasoning conformed to what moral theorists from Kant to Rawls had postulated as universal principles to guide ethical behavior. Once again, note that Kohlberg postulates the individual as the source of ethical judgment, and reason as the instrument of morality, although reason is now seen more in a developmental perspective.

The second school of thought on the ethic of justice finds its roots in Aristotle, Rousseau, Hegel, and Dewey. They placed society as the prior reality within which individuality develops. Furthermore, it is through experience, through living in society that one learns the lessons of morality. Participation in the life of the community teaches individuals how to think about their own behavior in terms of the larger common good of the community. In this school freedom is ultimately the ability to realize a responsible selfhood, which is necessarily a cooperative project. Ethics is grounded in deliberative practice within the community. Hence the protection of human dignity depends upon the moral quality of social relationships and this is finally a public and political concern. Citizenship is a shared initiative and responsibility among persons committed to mutual care.

From this perspective, a communal understanding of the requirements of justice flows both from tradition and from the present effort of the community to manage its affairs in the midst of competing claims between the common good and individual rights. That understanding is never complete; it will always be limited by the inadequacy of tradition to respond to changing circumstances and by the impossibility of settling conflicting claims conclusively and completely. Choices will always be made with sensitivity to the bonds that tie individuals to their communities.

Kohlberg himself believed that moral reasoning and choices were best made in a communitarian setting. He played an active role in the formation of "just community" schools. Hence, it can be argued that an ethic of justice, especially when focused on issues of governance in a school setting, can encompass *in practice* the two understandings of justice, namely, justice understood as individual choice to act justly, and justice understood as the community's choice to direct or govern its actions justly. In a school setting, both are required. In practice, individual choices are made with some awareness of what the community's choices are (school policies), and school community choices are made with some awareness of the kinds of individual choices that are being made every day in the school.

In a school that takes site-based management seriously, issues of the day-to-day governance of life in the school are inescapable. The ethic of justice demands that the claims of the institution serve both the common good of the community and the rights of the individual in the school. Ongoing discussions of student discipline policies, of faculty and student due-process procedures, of agreements about faculty time commitments, etc., are absolutely necessary. Furthermore, classroom discussions of issues within the curriculum will need to be carried on for the moral questions they raise about personal as well as public life in the community. Approaches to multicultural education should include not only the standard attempts to create better understanding of cultural differences, but also discussions of historical and present social conditions which breed unjust relationships between people of different cultures and explorations of ways to alter those social conditions. Issues of grading and testing could be examined from the perspective of justice, with such discussions leading to the development of alternatives to present practices that benefit some to the disadvantage of others.

No doubt freewheeling discussions of so many taken-for-granted elements of schooling will tend to get messy and unmanageable. Most educators dread such initial lack of definition. On the other hand, the debate is in itself educative. The only way to promote ethical attitudes and understandings about communal self-governance is to engage in it.

Deliberations about justice in the self-governance of the school, however, will benefit by recognizing varieties of justice. Ethicians distinguish between distributive justice, retributive justice and restorative justice. Distributive justice refers to the fair distribution of public resources. In civil society, the demands for distributive justice attend to the fair distribution of common public resources such as clean water, clean air, access to housing, access to jobs, rights to express oneself about public issues, rights to vote, equal protection under the law, access to public education, etc. In schools, distributive justice refers to issues such as relative equity in per-pupil expenditures in a state's public education system. Thus, a state is expected to provide a formula for equalizing the support students receive that the local tax base cannot provide. That equity in expenditures, however, is relative to the presence of a disability in a specific student, who by law has a right to access a public school education that provides special services to help that individual achieve a reasonably equal education. Retributive justice refers to the fair imposition of sanctions and punishments for violation of laws and public policies and institutional rules. In schools, retributive justice refers to punishments such as school suspensions for students who have violated rules against fighting or bullying, where it had been made clear to students and their families what those penalties would be.

More recently, school systems in the United States and other countries have developed a process of restorative justice. That process frequently requires that the offending student(s) (and often their parents) meet with the parties that have been wronged or offended by the student's behavior, and help the offender understand the damage or hurt that has been done, provide the offender an opportunity to seek some kind of reconciliation with those offended, provide the offender and the victim(s) an opportunity to discuss various ways the offender might restore or make up for the harm that has been done, having the offender agree to the terms of restoration, and settling on how the agreed upon restoration will be monitored and how the community receives the offender back into full membership in the community (Riestenberg, n.d.). Sometimes retributive justice is imposed along with restorative justice; sometimes restorative justice takes precedence over retributive justice. Since the 1970s restorative justice initiatives have spread to various countries, from Japan to Belgium to Canada and the United States. Beginning in 1989 New Zealand has made restorative justice the guiding force of its entire juvenile justice system (Zehr, 2002).

Evaluations of some restorative justice programs in schools suggest that the most effective ones are based on a continuous, proactive, whole school effort to build a foundation of community building around relationships of caring and respect (Morrison, 2007).

One of the limitations of an ethic of justice is the inability of the theory to determine claims in conflict. What is just for one person might not be considered just by another person. Hence discussions of what is just in any given situation can tend to become mired down in minimalist considerations: What minimal conditions must be met in order to fulfill the claims of justice? In his effort to improve on Rawls' theory of justice, Brian Barry (1973) introduced recent developments in economics and game theory in order to illustrate how two parties can negotiate an agreement over claims in conflict. The premise behind his lengthy and complex description of the mathematics involved in negotiating the agreement seems precisely to accept that very question, namely, what minimal conditions must be met to satisfy a just resolution to the conflict. In the example cited by Barry, it is a conflict between a rich person and a poor person. The reasoning involved assumes two isolated individuals, one of whom, by reason of his wealth, has more power than the poor person, and therefore can assume that the poor person will accept a resolution of the conflict that enables the poor person to get about 30 percent of the contested amount, while the rich person claims the other 70 percent. As long as the poor person agrees to the solution, it is assumed that the transaction is just. This notion of justice is not rooted in a sense of the common humanity that both share, nor any balance of the ethic of justice by an ethic of care—except by the supposed ethic of caring for the self. I will argue against this view of justice from two perspectives. One objection concerns the exclusive consideration of human life as a matter of economics and an economics of self-interest, at that. That perspective flies in the face of a view of reality as an interconnected and interdependent world, in which humans are seen as defined in their humanity by their responsible membership in this interdependent world. The other objection concerns the assumption of a morally neutral social and political world in which the economics of the market simply is what it is and is, in fact, the way it should be without any critical oversight by the human community that is supposed to be served by the market.

Grounding Care and Justice in the Human Condition

In attempting to reconcile the two different perspectives on ethics, a rather facile resolution relies on the claim that it simply reflects a feminine and a masculine way of looking at the world, whether the difference is due to biology or to socio-cultural conditioning, or a combination of both. Rather,

I suggest that there is an underlying root cause that affects the emergence of the tension between the two ethics. Rather than seeing care and justice as two distinct ways of looking at the moral demands of human life, I suggest that both men and women have to continually negotiate the tension between the two ethics in order to emerge with their personal integrity intact. In other words, males are not excused from honoring the demands of relationships simply because males tend to look at the world through a lens of separated individuals reasoning about the minimal demands of justice; neither are females excused from honoring the demands of justice because of their disposition to view the world through the demands of relationships.

This issue goes back to what was alluded to in the previous chapter, namely that contemporary science tends to confirm that the essence of every reality is its relationality.

The smallest physical particles are not constituted by their separateness, but rather by belonging to a field of energy, where everything in the field is related to everything else in the field in space and in time. As I understand it, that means that past moments in the universe-field are still being felt within the present dynamism of the field, and that distant occurrences are being felt throughout the field wherever in the field they might be recorded. The tendency of humans is to attend to what is present in both time and space without attending to how that present has been affected by and is embedded in the past, and how that reality in front of them may and will affect the immediate and perhaps a more distant future. When Henry Ford invented the automobile, who foresaw the impact of carbon emissions on today's atmosphere? Modern astronomy can detect the death and birthing of stars that have occurred million of years ago, but whose visibility is only now present to us through satellite telescopes. The setting of the borders of countries around the world after World War II is causing unimagined tensions in geopolitical relations in the present. With instantaneous communication available through satellite networks, what happens in a remote region of Tunisia sets off reverberations across all of North Africa and the Middle East, affecting stock markets in the industrialized nations, which affects fuel prices and causes me to alter my travel plans. The past moment almost a hundred years ago when my father decided to leave his home in Canada to come to the United States to seek employment where he met my mother is still reverberating throughout the lives of his children. And of course, my father's family's presence in Canada was related to a decision of their forebears to leave Scotland, which was related to the religious conflicts occurring in England at that time, which was related to..., which was related to..., which was related to.... Without all those past decisions, which were related to still past decisions, who and where might I be? Can I deny that I am embedded in a history that is still unraveling?

This more recent understanding of the natural world stands in contrast to a Newtonian view of the natural world in which isolated atoms interact with other isolated atoms to cause certain results in a specific place and at a specific time. The Newtonian view of how the world works supports a view of human society as made up of isolated individuals who interact with one another to cause certain results in a specific time and place. These isolated individuals, motivated by self-interest and governed by the evolutionary law of the survival of the fittest as well as the cultural assumption that "my community (my kind, my tribe, my class, my country, my religion, and, of course, my gender) represents the fittest," work out the rules of the social contract. That view of how the world works implicitly and sometimes quite explicitly runs through much of human history for the past four hundred years or more, with its attendant tragedies and marvels and realignment of the worlds of nature and culture and societies.

When one accepts the findings of modern science, namely, that we as humans are constituted not primarily by our separateness but by our *relationality*, our relationality not only to the whole human community, but also to the whole order of nature, and indeed, to the whole of history, we enter a world of interdependence and interrelationships. Such a view of ourselves and our world is still being absorbed by much of the industrialized West, even though it has been part of the culture and religion of much of the indigenous populations of the world.

If that perspective, however, is too much to absorb at one sitting, then, for the moment, let's reduce it to the human scale and confine our inquiry to the significance of our humanity as constituted by our relationship to other humans (Mitchell, 2000). Staying at that level then, one might begin to see that for every human, a given challenge simply by being human is to find out how this business of relationships works. In other words, the challenge is to discover how it is that I am both a separate, individual human seeking to establish an identity of my own, and at the same time I am in some sense in a surround of relationships with a responsibility to care for others, not only in my immediate family, but all kinds of other people. Not only am I supposed to care for others, but I discover that in my search for my own identity, I need to be cared for by others, not only by my parents and my family, but by all kinds of other people—the other children down the street, teachers, my school mates, the local policeman, eventually by my spouse and my children, insurance agents, doctors, pastors, tax collectors.

What this primordial challenge involves is to discover what "membership" means: how is one a member of the world? How do I belong to my parents and to my family? How are they mine and how am I theirs? As a family member I have family rights and responsibilities. Having rights means I can make demands on my family for protection, for a roof over my head, for food on the table and for a fair share of that food. But I also have responsibilities, responsibilities to care for my younger brother, to help with the family chores, to follow the family rules, to write my mom a nice birthday card. In the daily interaction within the family I learn how to care for myself and to expect care from my family and to return care to them. This isn't always easy because sometimes I care only for myself and this causes hurt or displeasure to those I'm supposed to care for. I also find sometimes that my family doesn't seem to care enough for me, me, me.

The situation gets trickier for both boys and girls when they go off to school. At school they have to deal with a whole bunch of kids they don't know, and they're afraid they won't fit in. What if the others see what klutzes they are, how they don't have a clue how to make friends. What if the teacher doesn't like them? In the playground, the older ones take charge of organizing games, so our newcomers just stand to the side and watch rather than participate; it's safer that way. They see some little kids getting pushed around by some bigger kids and they feel bad for the little kids but they don't intervene. They somehow belong to this school, but they don't know anything about the rules and responsibilities and the rights of membership. Finding out how to survive in this larger social environment is a full time job. Is that what membership means…survival?

This brief scenario of young children underscores the daily adventure in relationality whether for young girls or boys. They experience early on their desperate need to be liked, to have friends. Not having friends, walking around in crowds by oneself, wanting to connect with others but not knowing how, feeling vulnerable to letting others see one's insecurity, seeing others talking and laughing together like it's the easiest, most natural thing in the world, while at the same time terrorized by the supposed chasm separating oneself and the world these other kids occupy—these early experiences dramatize the need for relationships that seem such a risk to initiate.

There will be gender differences in the emerging pattern of accommodating to the challenge of relationality. For the boys in such scenarios they tend to be socialized into the male role of self-reliance, of surviving by asserting their autonomy. But that role tends to limit the experience of being cared for and the experience of caring for others. Relationships among boys will be established by the mutual acknowledgment among the boys of the talents and gifts each one possesses as an individual. Recognition of those talents and interests by other boys often leads to their forming a group to share and continue to develop those talents—the sports minded, the computer group, the technology/engineering/science club, the musical group, the counter cultural group ("Goths"), different hobby groups, the academics, and so forth. Their caring is not so much about the friendships emerging from group affiliation, but more the caring about the sport, the music, the latest computer "aps." Nonetheless, friendships will emerge from those groups as well. Often, girls are not invited to join those groups.

For the girls making friends will provide the security of acceptance, albeit within a web of intersubjectivity where being together is the most important thing. They can also form groups like the boys, but the conversations will differ, because being together is the more important thing than developing a competitive edge in mastering a skill or a technology. That does not mean that some girls will work at excelling in a skill or a technology. Sometimes, however, excelling is resented by the group. Being cared for and belonging to a group, can remove some of the motivation to become a person in one's own right.

Both boys and girls have to grow into the realization that caring for someone involves one's own subjective self relating to the other as a subject in their own right. As well, they have to learn to be cared for as a subject by a person who is a subject in their own right, rather than as an object for their own personal gratification or as a security blanket (Hollway, 2006). In other words, learning the lessons of relationality involves both emerging from the submersion of one's self in the other or in the group, as well as emerging from the focus on possessing the other as one's property.

While experiencing that the other validates one's existence as a subject of inalienable value, one has to gradually recognize that the relationship is a relationship of mutual validation. The other can only validate one if the other is a subject in her own right; one can validate the other's existence as loveable only if one is herself a person in her own right. The relationship brings gifts to the other even while the givers are also receivers simultaneously. The relationship should enrich the other both in his individuality and in his ability to enrich the relationship by his individuality. As will be emphasized in the following chapter, this flowering of the relationality of the human person follows a developmental pattern towards a fuller maturity—not automatically, to be sure, but as a strong possibility, given the right kinds of social and cultural supports, and some luck. As later chapters will indicate, the school has a definite role to play in supplying those cultural and social supports as it cultivates such development.

The Ethic of Critique

Up to this point we may be accused of spinning a tale of ethics that sounds too good to be true—the typical idealized theorizing of an academic. The real world faces us every day with pictures of violence done by dictators and their police, by tribal or ethnic rivals, by terrorists, by psychopaths. Furthermore, the misuse of power by governments, the media, financial institutions, corporations, professionals, the clergy, politicians, police, and others reveal a world riven with injustices and people who care only for themselves. Promoting the ethics of care and justice seems naïve when the world seems much more like a place for the survival of the fittest by any means, ethical or not. However, my response is that the media tends to report the bad stuff. The real world is also populated by many more people who daily do the right thing, who do their job with integrity, who raise their children with love and loyalty, who make sacrifices for others, who face up to the misuse of power. To be sure, there are people like ourselves, who live in the middle somewhere, who most of the time do the right thing, but sometimes cut corners, take the easy way out, accept "things the way they are," or simply avoid the extra step with the comment, "not my job." Still, the real world needs these citizens.

Educators tend to be people of hope. They are not blind to the apparent sorry state of public life. Their life's wager, on the other hand, is on the side of education, believing that working with the younger generation will better prepare them to join in the reconstruction of public life into something more humane and just. Nonetheless, one might also say that educators have not been assertive enough in embracing a third ethic that directly begins to confront the structural injustice that penetrates their own society and the educating process itself. That is what I call the ethic of critique. The enactment of this ethic can start in their own back yard and gradually move into a more ambitious long term effort in transforming the larger, institutionalized educational process.

It has become increasingly evident that schools and school systems advantage some and disadvantage others by the way they structure the learning, teaching, and assessment processes, by the resources they provide or fail to provide to various segments of the student body and the teaching staff. Hence an ethic for schooling appropriately includes the theme of critique.

The ethic of critique involves a process of assessing the institutional performance of the school from the point of view of structural justice and injustice. The adjective "structural" is meant to convey that the injustice is part of the way the school operates on a regular basis. The ethic of justice tends to attend to the interactions between two individuals involved in a specific situation. That situation exists within an institutionalized pattern which is not necessarily questioned; rather the concern for justice focuses in on the fair exchange within that institutional pattern. Thus, one can imagine a slave owner being considered just when he feeds his slaves well, provides decent housing for them, gives them Sundays off, and does not abuse the females. That measure of justice compares this slave owner to the others who treat their slaves badly in every respect. The institution of slavery, however, might not be questioned. The ethic of critique, however, attends to structures and procedures and policies that affect whole groups of people unfairly on a regular basis.

The ethic of critique should not be interpreted simplistically as an antagonistic, nit-picking effort of malcontents to find fault for the sake of finding fault. Rather, as an ethic it is concerned with promoting some moral good. In the case of education it is concerned to promote equitable treatment of all members of the school community in the way it systematically organizes and structures their work; in the way it systematically attends to the human, civil, and contractual rights of the members; in the ways it systematically protects them from or subjects them to psychological harm.

A critique, moreover, not only finds fault; it can also find virtue in the way a school operates. For example, a critique might recognize that a school has an excellent record of providing multicultural materials in its library collection, while at the same time it criticizes how the school systematically marginalizes minority parents of students in the schools. As the school community under the leadership of parents, administrators and teachers, faces the possibility of creating an ethical school, it may face the challenge to critique the structures governing the education of special needs students, or the policies of zero tolerance that require draconian suspensions for violations of a wide sweep of rules without allowing for any administrative discretion to consider extenuating circumstances. The critique will attempt to indicate the damage being done to different groups in the school and thereby open up the possibility of restructuring the way it treats those groups.

The ethic of critique developed here draws its force from "critical theory," that body of thought deriving from the Frankfurt School of philosophers (Adorno, 1973; Habermas, 1973; Young, 1990) and others sympathetic to their perspectives (Apple, 2004; Smyth et al., 2009; Spring, 2010). These thinkers explore social life as intrinsically problematic because it exhibits the struggle between competing interests and wants among various groups and individuals in society. Whether considering social relationship, social customs, laws, social institutions, power relationships, or language itself, these thinkers ask questions: 'Who benefits by these arrangements?' 'Which group dominates this social arrangement?' 'Who defines what is valued and disvalued in this situation?' The point of this critical stance is to uncover which group has the advantage over the others, how things got to be the way they are, and to expose how situations are structured and language used so as to maintain the legitimacy of social arrangements.

By uncovering inherent injustice and dehumanization embedded in the language and structures of society, critical analysts invite others to act to redress such injustice. Hence their basic stance is ethical for they are dealing with questions of social justice and human dignity, though usually not with particular, individual ethical choices.

Examples of issues confronted by critical ethics include sexist language and structured bias in the workplace and in legal structures; racial, sexual, and class bias in educational arrangements, and in the very language used to define social life; the preservation of powerful groups' hegemony over the media, and over the political process; the rationalization and legitimation of institutions such as prisons, orphanages, armies, nuclear industries and the state itself. The point the critical ethician stresses is that *no social arrangement is neutral.* Every social arrangement, no matter how it presents itself as natural, necessary, or simply "the way things are," is artificial. It is usually structured to benefit some segments of society at the expense of others. The ethical challenge is to make these social arrangements more responsive to the human and civil rights of all citizens, to enable those affected by social arrangements to have a voice in evaluating the consequences and in altering them in the interests of the common good and of fuller participation and justice for individuals (Freire, 1970).

This ethical perspective provides a framework for enabling the school community to move from a kind of naïveté about "the way things are" to an awareness that the social and political arena reflect arrangements of power and privilege, of interest and influence often legitimized by an assumed rationality and by law and custom. One can easily cite the critique of racially segregated schools, or the exclusion of children with special needs from most public, faith-based, and private schools. The theme of critique forces educators to confront the moral issues involved when schools disproportionately benefit some groups in society and fail others. Furthermore, as a bureaucratic organization, the school exhibits structural properties that may promote a misuse of power and authority among its members.

From a critical perspective, no organizational arrangements in schools 'have to be' that way; they are all open to rearrangement in the interest of great fairness to their members. Where unjust arrangements reflect school board or state policy, they can be appealed and restructured. The structural issues involved in the management of education, such as the process of teacher evaluation, homogeneous tracking systems, the process of grading on a curve, the process of calculating class rank, the absence of important topics in textbooks, the lack of adequate due process for students, the labeling criteria for naming some children gifted and others handicapped, the one-size-fits-all textbooks, time allotments for class periods, tests, semester courses—all these issues and others imply ethical burdens because they contain unjustifiable assumptions and they impose a disproportionate advantage to some at the expense of others.

The ethic of critique poses the fundamental ethical challenge to the school community: How to construct a school environment in which education can take place ethically? The ethic of critique reveals that the organization in its present form is a source of unethical consequences in the educational process.

Some would say that all organizations of their very nature tend in this direction. All organizations tend to make the rules and standard operating procedures the dominant force in organizational life, often smothering initiative, instilling fear of not being promoted or approved by one's superiors, severely limiting freedom of choice, reinforcing 'group think' and the official rationalizations for the way things are. On the other hand, organizations, paradoxically, are also places in the modern world where moral freedom and ethical creativity can be exercised in significant ways. It is in the restructuring of human institutions to meet the human purposes for which they were originally designed that one finds significant moral fulfillment.

Thus, educational leaders will face the continuing paradox of their institutional position in the school. On the one hand, they must acknowledge the tendency built into management processes to inhibit freedom, creativity and autonomy, and to structure unequal power relationships, in order to ensure institutional uniformity, predictability, and order. On the other, they must acknowledge their responsibility continually to promote that kind of freedom, creativity, and autonomy without which the school simply cannot fulfill its mission.

Hence the ethic of critique, based as it is on assumptions about the social nature of human beings and on the human purposes to be served by social organization, calls the school community to embrace a sense of social responsibility, not simply to the individuals in the school or school system, not simply to the education profession, but to the society of whom and for whom the school is an agent. In other words, schools were established to serve a high moral purpose, to prepare the young to take their responsible place in and for the community. Besides the legal and professional obligations, yet intertwined with them, the moral obligation of educator is to see that the school serves society the way it was intended. Hence, the challenge to restructure schools is a moral as well as a technical and professional challenge.

Two Questions

There remain two question, the response to which may close out this inquiry into a multidimensional ethical framework for educators. The first question involves the legitimacy of combining themes derived from three different ethical theories, despite what some might claim are irreconcilable differences among the theories. The second question deals with the practicality of the construct for educators. Namely, does it offer them a perspective that allows them to frame or name the most important ethical issues encountered in schools and to shape an environment that encourages ethical choice?

The three theories are not irreconcilable. They can be grounded on both the essential nature of human beings and on the essential nature of human society. That is to say, one can argue for the necessary interpenetration of each of them by the others if one is to argue for a fully developed moral person and a fully developed society. Even a superficial familiarity with the themes suggest that each theme implies something of the other theme: the ethic of critique assumes a point of view about social justice and human rights and about the way communities ought to govern themselves; the ethic of justice assumes an ability to perceive injustice within established

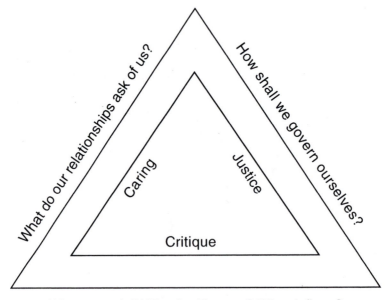

Figure 3.1 Basic questions addressed by each ethic.

patterns of the social order, as well as some minimal level of caring about relationships in that social order; the ethic of caring does not ignore the demands of community governance issues, but claims that caring is the ideal fulfillment of all social relationships, even though most relationships among members of a community function according to a more remote form of caring.

Moreover, each ethic needs the very strong convictions embedded in the other: the ethic of justice needs the profound commitment to the dignity of the individual person; the ethic of caring needs the larger attention to social order and fairness if it is to avoid an entirely idiosyncratic involvement in social policy; the ethic of critique requires an ethic of caring if it is to avoid the cynical and depressing ravings of the habitual malcontent; the ethic of justice requires the profound social analysis of the ethic of critiques in order to move beyond the naïve fine-tuning of social arrangements in a social system with inequities built into the very structures by which justice is supposed to be measured. The response to the first question, then, is that the themes are not incompatible, but on the contrary, complement and enrich each other in a more complete ethic.

The response to the second question is likewise affirmative. An educator's day is filled with ethical situations and challenges. Sometimes those situations clearly call for a critique of an unfair school procedure; sometimes they call for a sensitive guiding of student discussions of ethical issues embedded in the material under study; sometimes they involve debate over school policy in an effort to balance the common good with individual rights; sometimes they involve the demands of an individual person to be recognized and cherished for who she or he is. At other times, more complex problems require that the school board examine the problem from each framework, and perhaps balance the demands of all three ethics in its response to the problem. Given the focus of this book on cultivating an ethical school, the larger framework of all three ethical themes offers a more comprehensive and multidimensional foundation for such work. Figures 3.1 and 3.2 offer a visual diagram of how the themes work together to provide such a multidimensional perspective.

Conclusion

This chapter has attempted to develop a tapestry of ethical perspectives woven of three themes: the theme of caring, the theme of justice, and the theme of criticism. An ethical consciousness that is not interpenetrated by each theme can be captured either by sentimentality, by rationalistic simplification, or by social naïveté. The blending of each theme encourages a

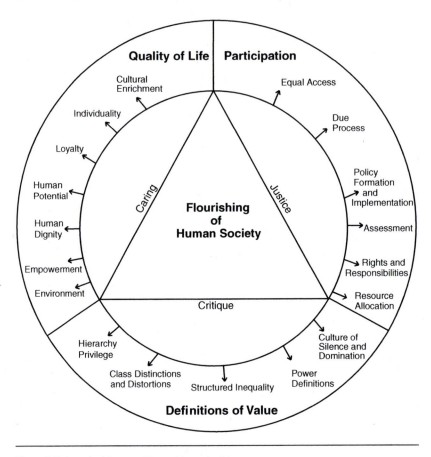

Figure 3.2 Important issues addressed by each ethic.

rich human response to the many uncertain ethical situations the school community face every day, both in the learning tasks as well as in its attempt to govern itself.

The ethics of caring brings us full circle at this point. Knowing our own failures to care for others, our own ways of rationalizing moral choices, our own reluctance to challenge questionable school arrangements, we are able to sympathize with the weakness in the human community. That weakness is part of being human. Despite our heroic ideals, we often act in distinctly unheroic ways. Hence a sense of compassion for our wounded and fragile humanity is needed for one who would act ethically, compassion for him or herself, and compassion for others. We have to extend our caring to forgiving. The forgiveness extended, we then go on with the business of making things right.

CHAPTER **4**

The Mapping of Moral Development

Introduction

The previous chapter laid out a perspective on adult moral behavior seen through a multidimensional ethical framework that combines three ethical schools of thought into an interdependent interpretive dynamic—the ethic of justice, the ethic of care, and the ethic of critique. The chapter, however, somewhat blithely presented a model of adult human beings incorporating these perspectives into their work as educators, as though this way of ethical living were relatively normal. The question this chapter asks is: How do adults become moral? Is moral behavior simply natural to human beings so that one could expect a two-year-old or a ten-year-old or a fourteen-year-old to express themselves morally the way adults do? Or, on the other hand, do children have to learn over several years how to become moral human beings? If children have to learn how to become moral, who or what teaches them the lessons about becoming morally adult? Is it the family or, as the saying goes, the whole village? Does this metaphorical village include the school? If it does not include the school, then what assumptions about schooling are included in that exclusion? If it does include the school, then what aspects of the schooling process carry this responsibility? Moreover, how does the village do its part? If families raise their children to be racists, does the village have a responsibility to present a different moral perspective about relationships between villagers of various racial backgrounds? Should the village and the school participate in a mutually reinforcing effort to raise moral children and adolescents? Who should set policies that explicitly deal with these mutually reinforcing efforts? This is a matter that is both over debated through a medium of simplistic opposites and under debated by easy assertions that the parents have the sole responsibility in this area. Many members of village school committees wish it would simply go away.

This chapter reviews some of the research and theory that attempts to illuminate the learning journey from childhood toward ethical maturity. Unfortunately, the research is hardly conclusive in answering the above questions. Subsequent chapters attempt to explore perspectives that might ground a reasonable response to these questions and that would support the cultivation of an ethical school.

Cautions and Distinctions

Before beginning this review, however, it is important to introduce some important qualifications. First, the research on moral development reviewed in this chapter is concerned with the *psychology* of moral development. The scholars involved with this research are psychologists, not ethicians. As mentioned in the previous chapter, there is a difference between ethics as a branch of philosophical studies and the study of the psychological dynamics of how humans develop into moral persons. Ethical studies deliberate philosophically about the meaning of "good" and "evil" in human affairs. Ethical studies attempt to identify the "good" intrinsic to moral activity, a philosophical analysis of what constitutes the good in being human, what contributes to the flourishing and sustaining of that good and what frustrates or diminishes that good. Philosophers can rely on psychological studies of moral development that point out how humans grow toward the formal embrace of ethical living; that point out how moral reasoning and moral motivation accompany the gradual choice to be an ethical person; that reveal how moral development can be arrested through inappropriate socializing influences in the young person's environment. Psychologists can rely on philosophical explanations of what human flourishing entails and match that explanation with their recording of the gradual psychological growth toward embracing forms of that flourishing in adulthood as part of one's definition of oneself. In that sense, psychological research on human and moral development can dialogue with ethicians' attempts to provide philosophical explanations of human flourishing, and of the frustration of that flourishing. For example, Kohlberg, a psychology scholar, references the consistency of his research (1981) with the ethical theory of the ethician, John Rawls' *A Theory of Justice* (1971).

Given an ethician's philosophical definition of human flourishing, psychologists can point out how humans develop (or fail to develop) toward that state of human flourishing. While considering what might constitute an education of humans that leads towards what ethicians and philosophers in general call human flourishing, therefore, it would seem most appropriate to study the results of psychological research into moral development in order to design an educational process that takes the journey of children toward moral maturity into account. When we do that, we recognize that the research on the psychology of early moral development takes us through what ethicians might call the pre-ethical stages of human development—though John Wall (2010) would insist that children are ethical, but in their own way, dealing with the challenges they experience. With findings from human development research in mind, then, the design of the education of young persons would focus on building a strong foundation during those years, a foundation that would predispose young persons toward embracing a fully mature ethical life in their adult years. Chapter two reflects an effort to relate the foundational qualities of a morally mature person to an appropriate approach to educating young people during the first twelve or so years of their schooling around the themes of autonomy, connectedness, and transcendence. Subsequent chapters will carry that effort forward.

The second point to note at the beginning is that the scholarly field of moral development is situated within the larger scholarly field of human development. That is, the perspective on moral development will reflect a relatively consistent match with the way the larger system of human development is conceived in psychological research and theory. What divides scholars of moral development often begins with or can be traced back to the way they conceive human development. The debates do not stop there, however. As Kurtines and Gewirtz (1995) deftly point out, theoretical interpretations of human development can be understood as belonging to clusters of theories of human development bonded together by metatheoretical *metaphors* that separate those clusters from other clusters of human development theories. Kurtines and Gewirtz (1995, pp. 9–12) posit five of these metatheoretical models labeled as: organic, psychoanalytic, behaviorist, contextualist, and dialectical. Theories of moral development, therefore, will exhibit inclinations to employ one or several of these core perspectives as they situate moral development within the larger framework of human development. To cite Kohlberg again, one might situate his theory of moral development within the organic cluster, following, as he did, the theory of Piaget (1971, 1975) on human cognitive development. We will see later on another example, that of Erik Erikson (1957), who embedded his notion of ethical development within his life-span theory of human development that combines an interplay of the organic, psychoanalytic, dialectical, and the contextualist themes of human development.

The third point to note is that the psychological research on moral development primarily focuses on the development of a moral concern with *justice*. These studies by and large are not concerned with the psychological development of caring, friendship, or loving. In contrast to the multidimensional framework that incorporates the ethic of justice, care, and critique espoused in the previous chapter, these psychologists are focused on the development of morality primarily as a concern for justice, and by and large ignore the ethic of care and even more so the ethic of critique. Though all would emphasize that morality is learned through social interaction, they focus on the development of a sense of cooperation, fair play, respect for the rules, reciprocity, and equity, as these moral dispositions are developed during the latency period of childhood. They do not spend much time on the earliest years of childhood, because those years are not primarily concerned with developing an ethic of justice. Instead those earliest years are concerned so much more with the interpersonal experience of giving and receiving care and love.

As was noted in the previous chapter, however, there has emerged a substantial amount of scholarly research on women's development as incorporating more explicitly an ethic of care (Chadorow, 1978, 1989; Fisher & Tronto, 1990; Gilligan, 1982, Hollway, 2006; Hollway & Featherstone, 1997; Noddings, 1984).

While calling attention to important developments in the research into women's ethical development, I must admit that I am a latecomer, if not an interloper, to this burgeoning scholarship. Nevertheless, I must add my voice as an educator to urge my fellow educators to attend to what this scholarship implies for the education of the young women in their charge. In the next chapter I will again address this issue.

Having noted the above points, we may proceed to explore what this psychological research might suggest to educators concerned to cultivate an ethical school.

The Psychology of Moral Development

Without going back in history to those great educators/philosophers who expounded on the human and moral development of children and youth (Plato, Aristotle, Rousseau, Pestalozzi, Montessori) and restricting our review to the last hundred years or so, we start with Jean Piaget (1971, 1975). Piaget's greater legacy involves his effort to map the cognitive development of children and youth from raw perception toward naming concrete objects and narratives, toward increasing levels of abstract understanding and thinking processes. His work in moral development echoes somewhat his mapping of cognitive development and the stimulation of disequilibrium occasioned by new experiences that would challenge earlier assumptions. He insists on the primacy of social experiences over moral reflection. According to Piaget social activity with peers precedes moral reflection rather than vice versa. At the same time, reflection on one's agency and its consequences may lead to new agentic initiatives. Piaget believed that justice lies at the heart of morality. He found, however, that children's responses to typical stories of children's experiences varied according to age and their moral development—from an external morality of physical appearances, to a pragmatic morality of tit-for-tat, to a more internalized morality that considered the context of the situation, the actor's intentions, and a more idealized sense of reciprocity (Gibbs, 1995).

The work of Lawrence Kohlberg began with his 1955 doctoral dissertation on moral development—a rather close "replication study of Piaget's findings" (Gibbs, 1995, p. 31). Kohlberg's findings, however, led him to enlarge the map of cognitive moral development to three overarching levels of moral judgment (pre-conventional, conventional, and post conventional), with two stages within each level, an earlier stage and more mature stage. His subjects revealed a more developed level of reasoning in late adolescence and early adulthood that identified morality (the morality of justice) with upholding the rules and laws of society as though those rules and laws superseded the rights of the individual. This "conventional" view of morality (Kohlberg's stage 3 & 4) has tended to be verified by later longitudinal studies. The empirical evidence for post conventional levels of moral judgment has been relatively skimpy, and Kohlberg himself has acknowledged that it is to be found in the rare individual (Buddha, Jesus, Gandhi) who appears to function at stage six—the living out of universal ethical principles. Rest et al.'s later work (1999) on moral development designed less rigorous criteria for post conventional reasoning and has thereby found a much larger population of adults who reflect post conventional moral reasoning.

Kohlberg further refined Piaget's insistence on peer interaction and the learning of cooperation as a stimulus to moral development by proposing a more general opportunity for role taking. That meant not only taking on the role of a peer, but taking on the role of various adults in society, adults who come from diverse backgrounds and function in diverse settings and circumstances. Kohlberg saw role taking opportunities as providing a gradual accumulating of cognitive dissonance or disequilibrium to stimulate a person to move beyond the reasoning of a less mature stage to a more mature stage of moral reasoning.

Kohlberg saw the educational implications of his theory of cognitive moral development. Working with a school system near his Harvard University home base, he helped to design and develop a model of a "just community school." This high school setting promoted student involvement in classroom and school-wide setting of rules and adjudicating disputes among students and between students and school authorities.

Kohlberg's student, Carol Gilligan (1982), as we saw in the last chapter, began a whole different tradition of studying the moral development of girls and women. Her focus on the development of a morality of care rather than a morality of justice drew needed attention to a complementary ethic. Gilligan herself, though accused of valorizing women's abilities and talents in the ethic of caring, saw the importance and clear possibility of the ethic of caring for both boys and girls.

Likewise, Hollway (2006), while exploring the intricacies of the caring relationship between mothers and their daughters, points out the importance of those early childhood learning experiences around caring for *both* male and female infants and their subsequent growth toward a more expansive maturity in giving and receiving care. She also asserts, citing Ernst (1997), that the process of separation from the mother, though gendered for both girls and boys, remains necessary for both if they are to be capable of an authentic giving and receiving of care between autonomous persons (Hollway, 2006).

James Rest et al. in their later work (1999), have situated the full development of moral judgment (he still holds out for the legitimacy and necessity of Kohlberg's distinctive emphasis on *cognitive* moral development across the pre-conventional, conventional, and post conventional reasoning) within a larger model of four complementary inner psychological processes. Those four psychological processes are: (1) *Moral Sensitivity* to the situation, a kind of empathy by which the person understands the situation as moral, imaginatively grasping how the persons involved feel, and the possible consequences of one choice over another; (2) *Moral Judgment* that considers which out of various responses would be most morally justifiable (the focus of his earlier research); (3) *Moral Motivation* to commit to the action judged moral and taking personal responsibility for the outcomes; and (4) *Moral Character* leading to persisting in the action despite resistance, fatigue and temptations (Rest et al., 1999).

Though they do not connect their findings to the work of Rest et al., there are echoes of Rest et al.'s model of the four psychological processes in the empirical research of Langlois and Lapointe (2010) who have been involved in studying how principals and district administrators in Canada respond to challenging ethical situations in their work. Through the use of the multidimensional framework of care, justice, and critique (Starratt,

1991), Langlois and Lapointe explore how their subjects name the ethical challenge they face. Furthermore, their study is not about the moral development of young people, but the explicitly ethical development of adult educators.

Rest et al.'s model of moral development, by including the affective dimension of empathy and sensitivity, presents an explicit corrective to Kohlberg's seeming privileging of reasoning as the primary, if not exclusive, motivator in making moral choices. Moreover, Rest et al.'s placing of the cognitive development of ethical understanding as but one of four critical variables in the development of the ethical person, responds to the criticisms of other scholars concerning the deficiencies in an exclusive Kohlbergian view of ethical development.

Rest et al., however, in my limited understanding of their work, do not seem to appreciate Gilligan's or other feminist arguments for the validity of an ethic of care. In one place where they take up the issue of gender differences (1999, pp. 115–116) they accuse the proponents of an ethic of care of dismissing the whole realm of macro morality (the concern for impartiality and nondiscrimination of justice to be found in laws and institutions governing public life) by contending that morality only concerns unswerving loyalty to face to face relationships—a gross misrepresentation of the feminist position on the ethic of care. Yet they simultaneously cite the fact that in the largest meta-analysis of fifty-six studies using their Defining Issues Test, it was found that gender accounted for a trivial variance in the scores. That would seem to indicate that women were able to reason about justice issues at least as well as the men. However, those findings still do not refute Gilligan's assertions about women's tendencies to focus on the importance of care, since their Defining Issues Test does not test for the presence of care, but rather for the reasoning around justice.

Their findings, in other words, confirm that the results of one's research reflect the kinds of questions the researcher asks. If he asks about people's development of an ethic of justice, but not about their development of an ethic of care, the findings will reveal the respondents' development of an ethic of justice, but not reveal anything about their development of an ethic of care. Langlois and Lapointe's (2010) research, by bringing all three ethics into their inquiry, surfaced respondents' sensitivity to all three ethics in various degrees among male and female educators of various ages and professional experience.

The Importance of Identity to Moral Development

In his research with children and youth, William Damon (1984) established a relatively clear distinction in the development of a moral personality. His research findings revealed two kinds of motivations for moral choices, what he called the morality of obedience and the morality of cooperation and reciprocity. In his research, the morality of obedience was an early phase of moral development in which young persons did what was considered the moral thing because adults demanded that of them. Adults imposed rules and guidelines for preferred behaviors. Obedience was rewarded by praise and other positive consequences. Disobedience was punished through various sanctions. Adult authority, or simply any exterior authority set the rules and the young person did the moral thing out of obedience, not out of any perceived moral value intrinsic to the activity. Through social interaction—games, parties, school events, family interactions—young people had the opportunity to experience the satisfactions of reciprocity and cooperation. Those social situations afforded satisfactions of being accepted, of friendship, of competing within agreed upon rules, of finding self-esteem through sharing in common efforts, in being a member of a team. The young person also learned the costs of selfishness, of not following the rules of the game, of letting the team down. Peers communicated various subtle and not so subtle negative feedback in response to their behavior. The young person learned the basic satisfactions of social participation with peers, in the absence of adult authority that imposes obedience. Damon concluded that as young persons enact cooperative and reciprocal engagement because they enjoy the experience, not because some external authority person is in charge, they internalize cooperation and reciprocity as the way they want to interact in the social world.

Damon found these young persons growing more and more self-directed, more and more owning their choices because that's the kind of person they wanted to be, because their sense of themselves, their identity was connected to being that way. On the other hand, some of the young persons in his research continued to act primarily in response to externally imposed rules, imposed by adults, or imposed by the peer culture. His longitudinal research of his subjects indicated that a significant percentage of them remained motivated primarily by externally imposed rules. Those persons tended to indicate that, if no one was present to observe their violation of a rule or law, and if there was little or no risk of anyone knowing, then they would feel free to disobey the rule or law. Others in Damon's research sample indicated that, whether or not anyone observed their behavior, they would obey the rule or law because it was the "right thing to do." They saw themselves as persons who held themselves to the standard of doing what was right; it was part of who they were, who they wanted to be.

Damon saw that the move between the two moralities of the child—from the morality of obedience to the morality of cooperation and reciprocity—tended to divide during middle adolescence as some began to connect being moral with their self-identity. Even then, the adolescent struggled for consistency, realizing that he or she does not always do what they know to be the right thing. His later research with Colby (Colby & Damon, 1992) confirmed his conclusion that only during the adult years do some people integrate their self-identity with their moral identity in such a way that they rarely have to give a lot of thought to what they should do because their moral sensibility is more thoroughly integrated with their self-identity, whereas in their youth their sense of self was not connected or very weakly connected to a moral self. However, Colby and Damon concluded that such a level of integration among adults seems uncommon (Colby & Damon, 1992). That conclusion tended to be confirmed by the research of Davidson and Youniss (1995) as they attempted to identify the moral development of fully mature ethical persons. Nonetheless, Colby and Damon confirm that there are some individuals who exemplify the fully developed moral person. Their research provides empirical evidence of the flowering of the psychologically ethical person. Their work tends to confirm the work of another scholar Augusto Blasi.

Blasi (1984) studied the degree of moral understanding of children of six years, twelve years and seventeen years. He found that children in all of these groups understood that certain actions were wrong, but that there were noticeable differences in their emotional responses to those wrong actions. Blasi concluded that the motivation to chose the moral course of action was lacking in the two early age groups whereas the older subjects connected moral choice with their sense of who they wanted to be, to their construction of their self-identity—a major task during adolescence.

Blasi indicated, however, that he was not denying the importance of moral understanding. He believed, rather, that it is the person who, in the intentional shaping of her or himself, chooses to embrace what he or she is understanding as a moral way of being. Like Damon, Blasi sees the motivational power to be moral emerging from the integration of self-identity and moral identity. For him, it is more clearly the self choosing to integrate moral sensibility into the way of being this person, rather than moral understanding persuading the self to act morally. Thus moral understanding is an activity of the increasingly self-constructing person, rather than an independent cognitional activity of the person that shapes the person. That is, moral understanding is something the person constructs through interaction with the world and under the influence, to be sure, of his socialization by the family and the culture. As that integration of the self and the moral identity it is choosing become stronger, so does the sense of moral responsibility for the self to respond to the moral demands of his or her world increase, leading to a strengthening of the link between moral understanding and moral action.

Larry Nucci (2008), an influential contemporary scholar of the psychological development of the moral self, has both incorporated some of Blasi's conclusions, and criticized other aspects of his work. He is concerned that Blasi and Damon are guilty of a form of reductionism, of reducing the complexity involved in moral development and moral action to a "moral self," a kind of person inside the person. Just as the term knowledge or cognition can be abstracted from the complexity of human consciousness and treated as somehow an independent thing or static reality that "causes" other things to happen in the person, so too, the term "the self" or the "moral self" or "self-identity" can be abstracted from the complex and dynamic life of the person and be treated as something in charge of an internal command center that operates independently of the person.

Nucci is referring to a danger that all scholars face who construct theoretical models to "explain" how a certain reality "works." All of these theoretical constructs are efforts to explain some of the intelligibility of a complex process in the social or natural world. These theoretical constructs reduce the reality they are explaining to a small number of variables that seem to be essential to the functioning of what they are trying to explain. So, Nucci is correct to warn us not to grant these theoretical variables a reality that controls and explains everything about the subject under investigation.

Nucci advises educators to recognize other variables at play in trying to understand the behavior of persons at any stages of their lives. An important variable is the cultural background of the person and its influence not only on the interpretive maps that culture affords for judging the value of one choice over another, but also its influence on the identity of the persons involved in the situations. The particular life history of the persons involved in the situation will also influence how they interpret present situations and how they respond to that interpretation. In some situations, the challenges are not moral at all, but might involve cultural traditions of deference, of face-saving, of traditional manners or customs that require observance, but not because they carry any moral significance. In other situations, Nucci would also agree with the proponents of social-emotional learning that affect and emotion play an influential part in developing interpersonal relationships. While recognizing that values play a part in moral decisions, it is the situation and its affective impact that winnows out whether and which values should or might come into play. We will hear echoes of that perspective in the next chapter that deals with Erik Erikson's model of the psycho-social development of the human person.

Women's Moral Development

Wendy Hollway, a British psychologist, has attempted to unravel the development of the capacity to care, taking into account the seismic changes occurring in gender relations, as well as multiple cultural and historical variables that influence the earliest childhood experiences of receiving and giving care (Hollway, 2006). Her research repeatedly reflects a sensitivity to unpredictable circumstances in the immediacy of the child's experience of the mother, as well as the immediacy of experiencing the invitation of others to receive the child's care. Nevertheless she declares to being grounded in a psychoanalytic perspective on the child's early experiences of intersubjectivity with the mother, in which, even before the advent of language, the child experiences care and expresses care in response. The consistency of the mother's communication of caring leaves an enduring impression, which, given the right confluence of a consistently positive experience of being cared for and of returning care, develops an *enduring* capacity to care.

Though obviously sensitive to the capacity to care of women, Hollway also proposes an interesting analysis of the young boy's developing the capacity to care. While the earliest caring by the mother leaves a lasting attachment to the mother, the boy's capacity to care as a male has to do with the caring negotiation of the *separation* from the mother, negotiated both by the mother and by the boy, with the mother encouraging a clearer self-individualization of the boy *as a boy* who has to become a subject in his own right. In other words, the boy is being released from the intimate intersubjectivity of his relationship with his mother and at the same time experiences a continuation of caring from the mother. Instead of having to aggressively tear himself away from a mother who doesn't want him to separate from the intimacy of the infant–mother fascination, the boy understands tacitly that he can separate from his mother and still be cared for.

For the young girl, however, while the mother still knows that she must let go of the daughter, the intense intersubjectivity (Mitchell, 2000) of their caring enables them to communicate in a deeper way for a longer time. Nevertheless, the girl also has to become a person in her own right. But a large part of being that person is being the mother's daughter. There is the assumption of imitation, where the young girl learns to be like the mother in helping her with the mother's family chores, as well as acting motherly with her dolls (while the brother plays with toy trucks and Pac-Man). That also calls for a certain imitation of the mother in showing affection and caring for the father. All of those experiences in the home tend to add to the shaping of her identity as someone who needs to be cared for (like her mother), and an identity of being a person who cares (again, like her mother).

The development of the capacity to care in the boy, while differing from the capacity to care in the girl, nonetheless is similar to the basic human development of both, namely that they develop a true self, become persons in their own right with an identity they can own and call their own. For the boy, however, the growing into an individual in his own right means becoming autonomous, self-directed, and independent enough to go out on his own and explore the world. The frequently unaddressed challenge for the boy, however, is to remain a caring person, and a person who interiorly knows that his destiny is going to be tied up with someone who cares for him. For the girl, becoming a person in her own right is tied up very much with being a person who is cared for and cared about and whose fulfillment will come through caring. The challenge for her is to fill out her identity by recognizing that her caring will be authentic if it brings her unique personal gifts to the caring relationship.

I believe Hollway brings out in her analysis of the development of the capacity to care the dynamic of relationality referred to in the second chapter. For both the boy and the girl, as well as the mother and the father, their full human development requires that they engage in the never-ending drama of performing themselves while performing their relationality.

Moral Maturity and Human Development

Assuming that educators can indeed cultivate an ethical school, that work must be consistent with the best of what we know about how youngsters learn to become moral and eventually embrace an ethical way of living. A large, life-span view of human ethical development, moreover, not only provides a perspective of the whole journey, but also illuminates how more mature ethical development implies and depends on earlier stages of the journey. Indeed, children pass through pre-moral stages where they learn rules and prohibitions but do not always understand why some actions are considered moral and some immoral. In other words they are relatively incapable of choosing on their own to be ethical. Toward early adolescence and throughout adolescence, youth are gradually coming to understand why some actions are considered always immoral (rape, torture, murder);

why some actions are considered moral or immoral depending on the circumstances (e.g., lying, killing, stealing), and why some actions are usually praised as being morally exemplary (acts of courage, acts of sacrifice for others, loyalty, keeping promises, defending the defenseless, caring for the elderly, the infirm, the homeless). That is to say, they are coming to appropriate and own ethical principles for living a fully human life.

The empirical research on moral development involves studies of early childhood into early adulthood and beyond, some of it centering on the cognitive development of moral principles, some of it concentrating on the transition from externally shaped and motivated choices and behavior to more internally adopted principles and a way of behaving that is tied to one's sense of identity. During the training of the child in the demands of social life, there tends to be little distinction between, on the one hand, teaching the child social conventions such as table manners, saying "please," and "thank you," avoiding slang and "swear words," and, on the other, teaching the child not to steal, to tell the truth, to avoid humiliating or bullying other children. As children mature into early adolescence they can tell the difference between the domain of social conventions and the domain of moral behavior (Nucci, 2008; Turiel, 2002). Unfortunately, some adults conflate adolescent rebellion against social conventions (length of the male's hair, proper attire for certain social occasions, musical expression, exploration of adult activity prohibited by society as inappropriate for adolescents) as ethical violations, either because of its implicit flouting of parental authority, or because, to the neighbors and religious authorities, it implies lack of "proper" parental socialization of their children. Educators need to resist confusing what are considered bad manners or violations of social conventions with ethical misbehaviors as they make judgments in their daily interactions with their adolescent students.

Summary

This chapter has attempted to summarize important aspects of the research into the moral development of the pre-adult years. The research points to the gradual development of habits of sociality, of early attempts to improvise on the drama of relationality. For both males and females, the adolescent years seem to comprise the crucial years for the gathering of earlier experiences into a more unified and consistent sense of personal identity, an identity that is concerned with an internalizing of the moral lessons learned over earlier years of development .

The chapter also surfaced the divide within the research community over an exclusive focus on the ethic of justice or on an exclusive focus on the ethic of care in the design of the very research questions that shape the findings and conclusions of the research. In the next chapter we will continue to explore ethical development through a more generous view of how that is embedded within a life-span of human development.

CHAPTER 5

The Geography of Human Development as Ethical Development

In the previous chapter we saw that scholarship around moral development tended to reflect at least tacit theories of the larger landscape of human development. This chapter will explore how the research and theory of Erik Erikson (1963, 1964, 1968, 1980) on the life-span of human development implies within it a development toward moral maturity. For educators, Erikson's theory offers a particularly appealing approach to cultivating an educational process that is both consistent with a view of life-span human development, as well as supportive of the ethical development of young people. I will argue that this approach to the ethical education of the young actually reinforces the integrity of the learning process as it engages the academic curriculum, as well as the more informal social and civic curriculum of the school.

In proposing the work of Erik Erikson as helpful in furthering the argument of this book, I am writing as an educator who has repeatedly encountered aspects of his theory echoed in the journeys of both students and teachers within the schooling process.[4] I am not writing as a scholar of psychoanalysis or psychology who is firmly grounded in the enormous scholarship of these fields, and who is therefore capable of providing a conclusive assessment of his place in those fields. Others, such as Cote and Levine (2002) and Roazen (1997), have attempted such a commentary. Neither am I embracing his theory as fully encompassing the human development of women as well as men. Furthermore, I would have preferred a more explicit integration of perspectives from critical theory in his work. I will attend to those limitations of his theory as the chapter unfolds.

His positive contributions to our understanding of human development as well as his shortcomings have been admirably summarized by the work of Carol Hoare (2002). My enthusiasm for Erikson's genius has been partially tempered by her summary of the points Erikson's critics have raised. I interpret Erikson's stages of the life cycle to apply to the development of *human beings* on their journey toward full personhood, males and females of all races and cultures. Despite Erikson's description of the stages of the life cycle from a male perspective, I believe that his stages of development can still apply to the development of young females, as long as the specifics of those stages would be adapted to apply more realistically, as well as optimistically to the development of young womanhood.

As for the criticism of his own cultural bias on his life-span theory of development, I can only refer the readers to his continued insistence on the contribution of the social and cultural environment of any particular historical period to the shaping of child rearing and socialization processes that can seriously limit or generously open the identity choices for young men and women. Identity formation is determined neither by parents, nor by one's class, gender, race, or culture, or historical moment. They all *contribute* to the way individuals respond to the matrix of circumstances facing them; they either facilitate healthy responses or encourage unhealthy responses. His point is that *now that we know* what contributes to healthy development and what contributes to pathological development, we ought to continually adapt our child rearing and socialization practices to open up creative and positive identity choices for the young (Erikson, 1974). I can only add my voice to his. *Now that we know* enough (even as we necessarily strive to know more) about healthy human development, we educators ought also to engage the young in a learning process that likewise opens up creative and positive identity choices for them—not only as individuals but as a whole generation. That is the rationale for advocating the cultivation of an ethical educational environment, modeling what we try to teach by the example of our own ethical development, and designing a curriculum that stimulates the ethical development of the young.

For now, recognizing that we cannot expect any one author to cover everything, let us concentrate on what Erikson suggests are important concerns for educators who want to cultivate an ethical ethos and practice in their schools. In what follows, you will read my "take" on what Erikson has to say, interpreting his analyses insofar as they might pertain to the argument of cultivating an ethical schooling process.

Erikson Within the Freudian Legacy

Erikson over the span of his clinical and scholarly work developed a kind of metapsychology of psychoanalysis. He expanded the focus of psychoanalysis from the captivity of Freudian perspectives to a life-span journey of the person. He translated Freud's Id into the biophysical embodiment of the person, insisting on the person's natural human existence as a body, rather than the body's domination of the person. He translated the Superego into the socio-cultural constraints on autonomy, seeing the child and young person potentially imprisoned in the dominance of family and society, tightly bound in the swaddling wrap of conformity to society's cultural, religious, and moral norms. Yet he likewise insisted that this socio-cultural Superego, while constituting a landscape for action did not, in a healthy human person, determine that the person must choose an identity that merely obeyed and replicated that landscape. Rather, Erikson argued that a healthy person could resist and transform elements of that landscape into a creative and innovative personal identity that claimed authentic existence within that landscape. His map of the healthy human life cycle indicates how humans develop toward maturity by meeting challenges presented to them by their larger socio-cultural world and by their embodied condition (Cote & Levine, 2002; Erikson, 1980; Hoare, 2002; Knowles, 1986). While Erikson acknowledged the force of libido, he tended to identify the challenges within the developing person as tensions resulting more from the cultural context of the child–parent relationship than the biological. For Erikson, the Ego, rather than the Id, is much more the source of agency in its *synthetic processes of making meaning*, and its *executive process of expression and action* (Cote & Levine, 2002). Depending on the severity and narrowness of adult controls through childhood—which eventually translate into the Superego—the Ego will enjoy more or fewer opportunities to act.

Erikson situated the human person involved from its fetal stage onward within the drama of a continually evolving self-realization in its interpersonal, social, and cultural relationality, gradually learning how to be a unique, integral, autonomous self while living out the blessings and challenges of one's biophysical, cultural, and social relationality. Erikson identified more specific challenges of that relationality as continually evolving, epigenetic challenges of human development, namely, the psychosocial process of bringing into ever fuller reality the person who is becoming a someone in relation to a historical cultural, social milieu. From a feminine perspective, one might say that the basic tension of relationality for women was seen as the problem of becoming an individual within relationships, whereas for the males it was more the problem of entering into relationships while attending to the importance of becoming an individual.

Erikson's extensive clinical practice of psychological counseling enabled him, within the basic heuristic frameworks of Freud, to identify the sources of his patients' pathologies in the frustration of normal attempts to meet the psychosocial challenges of childhood and youth development into fuller human beings. It led him to propose what healthy human development might look like if the passage through these challenges were more generously facilitated by parents, peers, other adults and institutions in the child's environment. As his experience as a clinician broadened with his study of human development across various cultures, so too did his reflections on the dynamics of healthy development as a complex psychosocial process of the individual's relationships with family, cultural socialization, and formal education. He began to see that the internal psychological growth of the person, while clearly related to the physical, bodily changes in the growing person, very much related to the socio-cultural surround and what *possibilities* for selfhood it offered as well as *prohibited* as interpreted by immediate family and formal education.

For Erikson, the resulting identity formation process was *both* the imposition of the possibilities and limitations by the cultural surround *and* the interpretation and *response* of the individual to them that created the decisive historical moments in self-identity formation, a moment or succession of decisive moments in the life narrative of the person. These moments were either successful realizations of a richer and expansive maturity, a greater ownership of one's authentic personhood, or a regression into a more childlike or infantile fixation and defensiveness. Depending on the severity of the defeat, the lasting results are minor or major, more easily reparable by more favorable moments of development or more resistant to further personal growth.

His theory of healthy human development pointed to a more mature enactment of one's relationality, moving toward a dialogical intimacy and into the mutuality of relationships of generativity. As one moved into a more mature enactment of identity, the giving and receiving of life to and from others becomes more and more a way of life, a deeper definition of the self, an achievement of Ego identity as well as a forecast of its further possibilities.

However, his interpretation of stages of development is very fluid, even its sequential pattern. Thus, the adolescent construction of identity is foreseen or reached out for in all the earlier stages of growth: identity formation begins with the trusting interactive relationship with the mother; it builds a foundation through the challenges of autonomy; it gains a broader view of the range of its possibilities through its initiation stage; through involvement with the games, the tools and technologies of society during the industry stage, it acquires certain capabilities in the elementary school years that feed the formation of identity. During adolescence all these earlier stages begin to fit into a more complex synthesis of the self's identity, often energized and focused by an embrace of ideals or ideology. That identity focus includes sexual identity which further prepares the young adult for intimacy and an exploration for a life partner with whom to raise a family. Thus, each stage of the life cycle presumes an already existing, preliminary base in early stages, even though each stage has its primary focus and proper challenge.

It is important to note the epigenetic metaphor embedded in Erikson's model of human growth. Just a flowers may be said to contain their flowering in their seeds, and then in their root and stem and leaf system, and finally in their budding stage, so in humans their future is contained in their fetal formation, their first years of infancy, their beginning years in school, and so forth. But in both cases, the external environment plays its part in supporting or inhibiting growth all along the way. Whereas, however, the plant survives or dies very much depending on its environmental network of supports, the human sapling has to make all kinds of internal adjustments in order to negotiate the construction of a self, a construction that relies and builds on a *symbolic* interpretation of the vagaries of its environment. As is evident in the pathology of the human in its complex improvisation of responses to perceived real or symbolic threats, the pathology reveals a psychological core of the person—the Ego in Freudian terminology—engaging in a mighty, if unsuccessful and self-defeating struggle of self-preservation, whose dramatic expression can reveal both a profound terror and uncontrollable rage at being denied its chance for a human life. That struggle is both a psychological and an existential (and therefore moral) struggle.

Based on his clinical experience with pathology, Erikson saw the struggle for a healthy development also as a moral struggle—to possess oneself rather than be possessed by forces in the environment. Erikson saw that struggle centered on the life-long struggle of the Ego for a human identity—an identity of self-worth connected to social validation as a somebody, as a real person, as a significant player in the historical realities of her or his life. This focus on identity Erikson gradually understood as a life-long, perpetually improvised achievement and ideal self-projection, the enduring moral agenda of the human person.

A Summary of the Life Cycle of Human Development

As all theorists must, Erikson (1963, 1980) employed heuristic categories to attempt to explain how human development occurs. We must remind ourselves that these categories are not things, but linguistic and conceptual tools for analyzing the complexities of human development. He distinguishes between the categories of the self, the I, and the Ego. The self (made up of various social and cultural selves playing out various roles) is the way the I and the Ego enact agency (Cote & Levine, 2002). The I is the periscope of consciousness, surveying the social–cultural terrain that contextualizes the arena for action, suggesting to the Ego what initiatives are called for. The Ego projects a self into action, employing the learned responses of the social role which the I will adopt. The Id provides the psychic energy, harnessed by the Ego in the service of agency. The Id's drive and instincts are there, but enculturated, so to speak, in roles. Thus, the Ego is the ground of the learning the I must go through as it enacts itself in everyday life.

At this point it will be helpful to gain a large perspective on the psychosocial learning process as Erikson understood it. He saw human development as a series of learnings about how one could manage one's own growth as a human being, in the process becoming more and more in charge of oneself, enlarging the sphere of one's agency, both physically and linguistically, imaginatively and willfully. Those learnings happened in a somewhat age appropriate sequence, beginning in infancy and stretching forward through young adulthood into mature adulthood, parenthood, career, middle and old age. He spoke of these learnings as being occasioned by a crisis, and here he continued with the vocabulary of his Freudian training (the Oedipal crisis, etc.) although he interpreted the term more as a challenge because, while it involves certain levels of stress, it is not perceived as a life-threatening crisis. Rather, humans experience life-challenges which must be met in order to grow into more mature human beings, challenges which are met in various degrees of success over the course of a specific range of years in a person's development. The severity of these challenges depend on the flexibility or rigidity of the familial and cultural environment as well as the physical and psychic endowments of the person, and how well the person has met the earlier challenges in her or his human development.

These challenges begin during infancy with the *challenge to trust* the mother's constancy of care and attention to the infant's basic needs. That trust in the mother lays the foundation for trusting other human beings in one's life, and for trusting the basic beneficence of one's world. It also establishes a foundational understanding that *one's life is inescapably relational,* that independence from relationships is not an option for a healthy and satisfying human life. Erikson emphasizes that each stage or life-challenge has a healthy or an unhealthy outcome, or, in most cases, a *relatively* satisfactory or unsatisfactory outcome. These outcomes, as we will see, are not necessarily definitive in fixing a person's development irrevocably. One can repair the damage, so to speak, through more positive experiences in later stages of one's life, through experiences that enable one to revisit the challenge perhaps now more intentionally. Likewise, success at one stage does not guarantee continued success in meeting future challenges.

Many parents are familiar with the "terrible twos" when children begin to assert their autonomy, often in frustrating and unpredictable ways. The child's most frequent response is, "No." (I won't do what *you* want. *I'll* do the choosing.) Though Erikson did not go into how female children go through this stage, he would have acknowledged that the general sociocultural surround of the family would dictate what kind of autonomy might be granted to young girls, and what kind of autonomy might be granted to young boys. In their *human* development, both boys and girls have to learn what identity choices as an autonomous person are available and what identity choices are inhibited within their social milieu. For both boys and girls going through that stage it is a risky business.

To move into the next stage, initiative, as their physical mobility and language mastery develops, the relatively autonomous child will then begin to explore the limits and boundaries of her or his environment, both physical and imaginary, cultural and sexual. Again, the child takes the initiative in exploring the various *relationships* within the environment, relationships that continue to communicate information about the social expectations of the immediate family and community that provide for satisfying mutuality of relationships. The enactment of this stage would be likewise nuanced by the gendered possibilities open to the child. In more tribal or feudal societies those possibilities would be more constricted for both males and females.

As the child experiences primary and middle school during the traditionally labeled "latency" years, the youngster tries out a variety of tools, and tool using processes, whether those involve sophisticated technology (computer games, chat rooms), craft or artistic tools (playing the piano or the guitar, computer graphics), athletic skills (dribbling a soccer ball or basketball, playing hop-scotch or skipping rope), or a range of hobbies (stamp collecting, boy scouts, girl scouts, co-curriculars at school). During these years the youngster is finding out what she or he can do well, what natural talents or interests can be mastered. These learnings will further enlarge the child's sense of self and of the various ways she or he can *participate in the life of the community*. During the teenage years, youngsters

Table 5.1 Life-cycle challenges and strengths to be developed

Stage	EGO Development Outcomes	Resulting Strengths
Infancy	Trust vs. Mistrust	Drive + Hope
Early Childhood	Autonomy vs. Shame	Self-control, Courage, Will
Play Age	Initiative vs. Guilt	Purpose, Imagination
School Age	Industry vs. Inferiority	Method + Competence
Adolescence	Identity vs. Role Confusion	Devotion + Fidelity
Young Adult	Intimacy + Solidarity vs. Isolation	Affiliation + Love
Middle Adulthood	Generativity vs. Self-absorption or Stagnation	Production + Care
Late Adulthood	Integrity vs. Despair	Wisdom

now begin to explore a variety of life-long choices about who they want to be as adults. Career explorations help to expose them to a variety of adult roles; strong attachments to role models emerge; sexual identity becomes solidified as rapid physical maturity makes them acutely aware of their sexuality and their sexual attractions.

As the adolescent moves into young adulthood, the exploration of identity matures into a more intentional choice of an identity-trajectory of her or his life. Within Erikson's theory, he does not go into the female identity. As I read him, his treatment of identity tends to reflect much more of a male identity formation than a female identity. For the male, this development in young adulthood completes, in one sense, the whole struggle of a young person's first third of his life, namely a struggle to construct and be true to a self, a self that is consistent and reasonably predictable. This struggle will gradually lead the young adult to the point in his life *when self-transcendence is possible*. Having a reasonably clear grasp of himself, it is now possible to let go of the *exclusive concentration* on becoming a somebody. Now it is more possible to give the self away, to give *from* the self, to give *of* the self—in short, to transcend the self in *reaching out* to bond with another, or with a cause that is much greater than self-development.

From my limited reading of feminist literature, I would suspect that, especially in more conservative and tradition-bound cultures, the dynamic of self-transcendence for females would have started much earlier, and would be woven into their identities throughout the earlier stages of their development. In contrast with the males, the Eriksonian identity stage for females would tend to reveal the tension between relationships and the emergent need to be much more a subject in her own right, not so much to claim independence—though that might enter into the equation—but rather, to be able to be more fully oneself in the relationships of intimacy as well as in the various roles as care-giver. Given the multiple voices and perspectives about women's development, it is necessary to avoid any simplified attempt to name the experience of all women, whether in tradition-bound cultures, or in more open and flexible cultures.

Conn (1977) argues that Erikson's mapping of human development enables a clear delineation between the "moral" (following adult-imposed rules) or pre-ethical stages that precede young adulthood, and the self-transcending identity-choices involved in mature intimacy and generativity and integration. In the earlier stages one is focused primarily on the self. Although there are obvious relationships of mutuality to be negotiated, the focus has been primarily on "what's in it for me?" As one enters into intimacy and generativity, one is clearly involved in a form of acting out of care and beneficence for others which is so naturally identifiable as a virtuous form of human activity. Even here, however, it is easy to detect an assumption of the male perspective in Conn's interpretation of Erikson. One might argue, for example, that girls move toward that sense of transcendence earlier than boys, precisely because their identity formation has been tied to the ethic of caring and the identity of care-giver.

Where the next stage, or life-challenge emerges, namely the move towards intimacy, we see the male self-transcendence unfolding. I interpret Erikson's treatment of this stage as reflecting an assumption of the male perspective. For both males and females as human beings, however, intimacy does not mean self-annihilation or self-abandonment. Rather it means the meeting of two autonomous, humanly mature adults in a mutual invitation to share life together. They enter into a new experience of themselves in their relationality. They find themselves by entering into the reality of the other, and become more real as they see themselves in the eyes of the other. In marriage, that sharing involves (potentially, anyway) as much as is humanly possible. In relationships of deep friendship and loyal companionship, that sharing may not involve such totality of daily living together, including the responsibilities of child rearing. The point here is that having a clear sense of identity that one chooses and intends to be loyal to enables the *fully mature human* to emerge. The fully mature human is now able to share the full nakedness of their person with another in intimacy, but is also able to generate new life. That new life is the life of "us." In the generation of that new life, the fully mature humans embrace the responsibilities to nurture and care for that new life. The generation of that "us" lays the foundation for the generativity of parent-hood. The simple physical generation of new life has to be carried forward to the protection and growth of that new life in its own journey toward full selfhood.

As one moves into the generativity stage of human life, there are other demands to transcend self-interests in order to contribute to new life within the civic and occupational communities one belongs to. At its most basic level, generativity involves the many sacrifices of self-interest and self-gratification required in one's partnership with the other, and in the work of parenting and one's work in a career. The generativity challenge of the work in a career entails going beyond the bare minimum to a larger effort to contribute something of genuine value in that work. Generativ-ity can involve generating inventions, negotiating new political policies, creating works of art, writing scholarly books, teaching young children in school, healing sickness through the healing professions, building a bridge, bringing criminals to justice, conducting research on new medi-cines, preaching inspiring sermons, and, indeed, being a nurturing foster parent. Generativity is an exercise of human virtue that extends over the last half or last two thirds of a person's life, even during retirement, and can be exercised in a multiplicity of ways by the same person enacting vari-ous social and cultural roles.

Finally, there is the stage or life-challenge of bringing one's life into some kind of integrated whole. That challenge involves a gradual accep-tance (not without pain) of the totality of one's life, its joys as well as dis-appointments, its triumphs as well as its less than courageous moments, its mistakes as well as its satisfactions. All of one's experiences come to be seen somehow as necessary for one to have learned the many lessons life has to teach, to have arrived at the completion of one's journey, where the truth is that the journey, rather than the destination holds the truth about oneself. This life-challenge leads to a form of wisdom, a wisdom that can be passed along in a final form of generativity. While this view of the last stage of human development was a product of Erikson's middle age, he later expressed the opinion that it was too optimistic, that it did not take sufficient account of the physical and psychological deterioration involved in the elder years. Even then, he went back and forth on the importance of reasserting the trust in the life process.

Cautions Against Simplification

The above map of Erikson's understanding of the life cycle can induce several misinterpretations. One major misinterpretation is to see the map as expressing a static, once-and-for-all sequence of challenges resulting in either-or outcomes. First, the outcomes of engaging a life-challenge do not issue in a complete victory or complete defeat. Rather, the results will tend to be more-or-less success or more or less failure. Depending on the quality of the maternal interactions, a child comes to trust either more completely in the adult world, or to recognize that sometimes one's trust is disappointed, even though, by and large, in most circumstances adults and the world in general can be trusted to be predictably responsive to one's expectations. That trust makes it more likely, though not inexorably guaranteed, that young persons will be able to bring that trust to support their drive for greater autonomy. That is to say, youngsters have an intuition that their drive to be more independent will not turn the parents (whom they have grown to trust) against them in a punitive rejection. So the struggle to gain autonomy, while frustrating for parents, is not a rejection by the child of the fundamental relationship of caring dependence. Rather, if the relationship is to grow into something more human, the child has to own itself in increasingly insistent agency in order to be in a *more genuine* relationship with the parent. This example also illustrates that the virtue of trust developed in infancy must itself be transformed into a more complex and deeper trust that will sustain the relationship even in the conflict of wills. Thus, it becomes apparent that in this developmental sequence of challenges, the prior learnings will become incorporated into the learnings called upon by the newer challenge; the earlier learnings are both *required* and further *deepened* in the new challenge.

Of course, success at one stage does not guarantee success at the next stage. A mother might be very devoted to caring for her infant's needs. However, the relationship of total dependency may have become very pleasing to the mother, a relationship the mother doesn't want to change. The mother can react very strongly against the child's initial attempts to have its way. The mother can communicate that the child ought to be ashamed of itself for opposing the mother, after all she has done to provide for its care. Thus we can see how the parent can shame the child for being disobedient and rebellious, inducing the child to retreat into a more passive response to her in order to retain at least the earlier relationship with the mother. However, the mother has inhibited the child from entering into a more mature relationship with her. The mutuality between them will be reduced to a more one-sided relationship. Indeed, as a result of the mother's resistance to the child's desire for autonomy the child's earlier sense of trust will likely be diminished as the child copes with the alternating feelings of resentment and shame.

Stages Within Stages Throughout the Life Cycle

The progression through life-challenges is not a once-and-for-all sequence. As one enters into very new experiences, say, moves into the first job as a teacher, it may very well be necessary to apply the sequence of earlier learnings all over again. That is to say, the neophyte teacher may have to learn whether the new environment and the new relationships are trustworthy, or at least to find out whom she can trust among her teaching colleagues, and how much she can trust the principal, and how much of a trusting relationship is possible with her students. With some positive results in that search, the teacher may be able then to explore how much autonomy is possible in her work. From there she may move on to explore the boundaries of her work and of her relationships with her colleagues and students. Besides teaching, she might explore other relationships with her students as a coach, or a moderator of a co-curricular activity. With those initiatives resolved, she may then be ready to go to work on gaining new skills and competencies in order to broaden her professional stature in a replay of the industry stage of her development.

Another example would be in the initial stages of an intimate relationship. How much trust to invest in the potential life-partner? How much of one's true self will be revealed; how much autonomy will the other tolerate? At the start, what boundaries will be set, what new interpersonal landscapes will be explored? What kinds of new skills (budgeting, cooking, child care, home repairs, etc.) will need development? What kind of parent identity will I adopt?

Thus, it becomes apparent that the stages of development will have repetitions at later times in the life cycle. It also warns us that the terminology of "stages" can be misleading if it communicates a rigid compartmentalization of human development. Rather, that vocabulary should be understood as a useful tool for analyzing the kind of challenge a person is facing, a challenge that is particularized by age, physical development, gender, culture, occupation, family situation, and so forth. Nevertheless, Erikson's interpretive framework illustrates the intrinsic logic to the dynamic and progression of challenges: trust allows for autonomy, which provides a foundation for initiative leading to industry, and so forth.

Erikson's map of human development presents us with a large *ideal-type* picture of development into a fully mature humanity. That map is neither a denial nor an explanation of evil or human folly, although through it we can understand how the frustration of healthy development can lead to a diminished humanity that translates infantile rage or jealousies or role confusion into sick or inappropriate choices. Nevertheless, there are many humans who have been humanly crippled in their early development who live relatively harmless lives, for whom the boundaries provided by society keeps them more or less in line with the majority of their neighbors. With them, it is more a question of *what they might have become* with greater encouragement in their development, rather than dismay over their behavior.

With these cautions about simplified readings of Erikson's map of the life cycle, we can now turn to an analysis of the psycho-dynamics of the learning process that takes place every day as the person both fashions and engages his or her "true" self. At this point we are better prepared to *link* this learning of how to meet the challenges of growing into an increasingly mature person *with* the learning process involved in engaging the academic curriculum of the school.

Linking School Learnings to Life-challenges

When school learnings in the academic curriculum introduce young people into the intelligibility of the worlds of nature, of culture, of society; into their relationships with those worlds, and into their participation as members of those worlds, the school is tacitly suggesting ways to play out the social and cultural roles called for in such participation. Those roles should not be externally superimposed on the learner; rather, they should emerge through the learning process as enactments of relationships which each world contextualizes in the activity of participating in it. By enacting the relationship to those worlds, I mean *both* understanding those relationships *and* responding to what those relationships imply. Moreover, the enactment of the relationship is usually exploratory at first, and becomes routinized as the feedback of "fit" with expectations of the world becomes, for that individual, the gradual and flexible adoption (usually quite tacit) of a role as a member of that world.

Sociologists and social psychologists, finding broad similarities among the enactments of large numbers of individuals, classify those similarities as roles. "Role" is a metaphor derived from the theater, where actors perform the role of servant, jealous husband, arrogant bureaucrat, favor-currying sycophant, flirtatious female. Sociologists and social psychologists use the term in a more general sense, diluted of much of the theatrics, to describe behaviors one might observe in "ordinary life"—the role of mother, husband, consumer, political conservative, feminist, car salesperson, professor (Goffman, 1959). Roles can apply to gender, ideology, profession, economic activity, class. They are ways the self is socialized into behaving. What makes human life interesting, if sometimes annoying, is that the individual always gives her or his own individual twist or nuance to how a role is enacted in a given circumstance.

In Figure 5.1, we have a visual image of how the Ego is the core of the individual, making sense, at an unconscious level, of the information it receives from the I at the experiential level. The I functions at the surface of the individual, at the level of consciousness, of sensory experience, of behavior and social interaction. The I is organically and dynamically connected to the Ego which is below consciousness.

The Ego is the collector of the residue of a lived history, of the hurts, joys, satisfactions and disappointments experienced and interpreted throughout that history. Those joys, hurts and disappointments have been interpreted through the filters of the body (its needs, drives, sensations, feelings), and through the filters of the Superego (what parents want, encourage, forbid; what the culture approves, disapproves, sanctions, rewards; how religion interprets God or the gods and one's relationship to the transcendent).

The I tells the Ego what is "happening" in the immediate, experiential world, and the Ego tries to make sense of that initial Gestalt of what is happening—sometimes successfully, sometimes incorrectly, sometimes bewildered or confused by the surface context, sometimes finding mixed value messages as the experiential world is filtered through the Superego. Through that interpretation, the Ego scripts and clothes the general response of a self that corresponds to the situation. That response is a response to the initial intelligibility the Ego makes of the situation (synthetic processing) and also an expression of what the Ego wants to do in the situation (the executive processing), what the Ego wants out of the situation, what the Ego senses is appropriate and consistent with the deepest intuition of who the person (the whole person—Ego, body, cultural member, the social self, the I) *is*.

In order to grasp the *deep connection* of understanding (the cognitive aspect of learning) with responding (the affective, willful side of learning), we have to examine Erikson's understanding of the Ego as *the source* of both understanding and agency. Note that the Ego is the source *both* of understanding *and* of will and action. This point is often missed in the psychological literature that tends to locate understanding in "the mind." "Mind," however, is as much an abstraction as is "Ego." Both are heuristic categories used to interpret and explain the functioning of human beings. The category of mind, however, often connotes an impersonal processing mechanism, separate from emotion and affect, which are interpreted as found in "the body" (as in mind–body dualisms, often found in the advice, "Think with your mind, not with your body."). By placing the activity of sense-making, of meaning construction in the Ego, Erikson is suggesting the immediacy of knowledge to the person, *within* a unity of knowledge, affect, and choice, each interpenetrating each other and influencing each

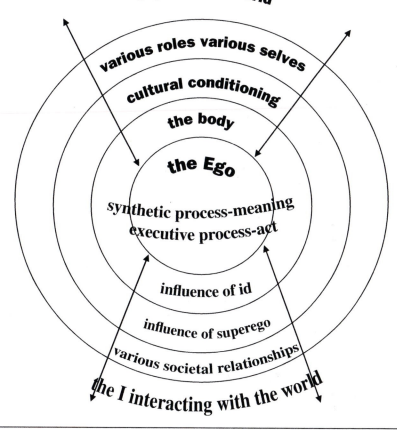

Figure 5.1 The influence of the Ego on meaning making and action.

other, even as they are filtered and expressed by social roles, bodily dispositions, and cultural values.

The heuristic model in Figure 5.1 (and we must remember that we are using interpretive categories to interpret the way we think a person "works") indicates that the process of meaning making, which is the essential core of everything we call learning, is affected by being filtered through successive layers that have come to constitute the rich structure of the human person. Those filtering layers include not only the immediacy of perception, but the consciousness of various social roles the person has been socialized to play, as well as the cross-hatching filter of cultural structuring by language, value and belief orientation, religious and parental teachings lodged in the Superego, and the instinctual and genetic predispositions of the body. While knowledge implies intelligibility, in this model it implies a very complex construction, probably synthesized over varying periods of time, built out of multiple internalized influences. That may explain why the initial impulse of the young learner (and often of adults) is to embed what he or she knows in a story, rather than in an abstract definition or a formula. In its story form, knowledge is more personal and is constructed out of numerous experiences and associations.

Because of Piaget's bias toward science and mathematics, he ranked this narrative kind of cognitive processing, which he called "concrete-operational thinking," as a less mature form of thinking than "formal operations"—the use of abstractions to think about other abstractions, following the rules of formal logic. Formal operations may be the more desirable level for scholars and professionals to employ, but is rarely found as the consistent mode of thinking even of 12th graders (Sprinthall & Theis-Sprinthall, 1983). Indeed, some research suggests that only about 30 percent of adults use some aspects of formal operations, and those adults belong to modern societies with complex technologies that require such levels of thought (Bart, 1977, referenced in Sprinthall & Theis-Sprinthall, 1983, p. 23).

This research does not lead me to argue against the desirability of attaining formal levels of thinking, nor, indeed, that the narrative way of making sense, though perhaps humanly richer than abstract, logical thinking, is always more appropriate. Instead of claiming superiority of one way of thinking over the other, why not simply say they are different? One way of thinking might be more appropriate and effective in given circumstances than another. Sometimes both might be employed as reinforcing the mutual cogency of the other expression. The widespread insistence that schools should emphasize higher-order reasoning as the exclusive or primary criteria for quality learning should be questioned. In other words, I wonder whether the attempt to short-circuit the slower, but more authentic process of learning which Erikson's model suggests, results in a process of learning that is so truncated and speeded up as to eviscerate the rich and lasting quality of learning that is normal—that is, learning tied to the Ego development of the learner. Does enacting the role of "student" in K-12 schools, under the ever present pressure to produce "right answers"—the definition of school achievement—gradually lead the learner to reproduce for and in that role a form of make-believe learning that satisfies the role expectations of school authorities, but is completely disassociated from the agenda of the Ego to define who one is or wants to become (Bonnet &

Cuypers, 2003; Wiles, 1983). This disassociation, which is actually, if tacitly, encouraged by classroom routines, may explain the testimony of many students who characterize the learning process in schools as alienating, unreal, and meaningless (Shultz & Cook-Sather, 2001). In this regard, I can cite not only the critical reflections of John Dewey, but also of Applebee (1996), Becker (1971), Bruner (1987, 1990), Egan (1990, 1999, 1997), Hogan (2010), Macdonald (1971), Reay and William (2001), and Seymour Sarason (2004), among others as largely of this opinion.

Connecting Learning With One's Journey Toward Authenticity

In schools, learners are socialized into acting out the role of "student." Often, if not always, the role of student is to listen passively to the explanations of the teacher, to absorb passively the information in the textbook, to find the answers to the questions or problems at the end of the chapter by going back through the chapter to find the exact wording that corresponds to the question or problem. The material under study is not required to be connected in any way to the student's experience, or to his or her life-world. The academic curriculum tends to be a world unto itself, arranged in its own logic and vocabulary and abstractions. Mastery of that curriculum is equated with a more or less exact repetition of what the teacher or the textbook said.

Erikson placed great importance on Ego identity, on the Ego's sense of its own consistency throughout multiple and varied experiences, and on its ability to act consistently with its past knowledge and understandings as well as its interests, wants and desires, and in response to the apparent demands of the present situation. Thus, one can begin to understand from a psychological standpoint (illuminated by the categories of Erikson's psychosocial model of the individual) the significance of Charles Taylor's *ethic of authenticity*. Taylor (1991) maintains that the construction and enactment of personal authenticity is the most fundamental and profound ethical responsibility all human beings face. Erikson and Taylor help us to understand the demands of authenticity. To own oneself, to sing one's song, to improvise one's place in the drama of life, to be real instead of phony, to be a somebody instead of a cardboard character mouthing a script someone else has provided, is to be responsible to the truth of who one is, has been, and is capable of becoming, and to the truth embedded in one's relationality. Being real, being authentic is the burden only each individual can bear, is the adventure only the individual can live, is the satisfaction and fulfillment only the individual can enjoy. The drama of authentic individuality, however, always involves the intrinsic relationality of the individual and the worlds she or he live in. Those worlds both gift the person and limit the person as she or he enacts that drama.

Make-believe learning in the pursuit of someone else's approval, when reinforced over twelve to eighteen years of schooling, induces a habit of mindless inauthenticity.

When young people are exposed to inauthentic learning for twelve or more years then it is little wonder that at the final bell of every day, and on the last day of school every year, so many young people depart with such feelings of emancipation. They are free to be themselves. Despite their acceptable test scores, however, their relationships to the natural, social or cultural world remain impoverished, and thus, they hardly know who they are. And if that is true, then we as a society and a culture are bound to live with the consequences of that colossal mistake.

The understanding of learning as involving both Ego development as well as cognitive development is, by and large, absent from the discourse about the school renewal process. It is the 500-pound gorilla sitting in the classroom that is consistently ignored by the field. In any community's effort to educate its children and youth through late adolescence, in the process of preparing them to participate in the ongoing life of the community as involved stewards of the common good, as productive workers who contribute to the community's sustainable prosperity, and as sociable and affable neighbors who share the public resources in just and responsible ways—that educative endeavor must promote a learning process that cultivates a deep and broad understanding of the interconnectedness of humans to their natural, cultural and social environment, and engage learners in a gradual participation of responsible membership in those environments. That kind of learning is the kind of transformative learning our society desperately needs.

At this point I want to repeat verbatim an earlier paragraph expressing how I understand Erikson's insistence on the *centrality of identity* to the life journey of the individual.

Based on his clinical experience with pathology, Erikson saw the struggle for a healthy development also as a moral struggle—to possess oneself rather than be possessed by forces in the environment. Erikson saw that struggle centered on the life-long struggle of the Ego for a human identity—an identity of self-worth connected to social validation as a somebody, as a real person, as significant player in the historical realities of her or his life. This focus on identity Erikson understood as a life-long, perpetually improvised achievement and ideal self-projection, the enduring moral agenda of the human person.

Here we come to a decisive moment in the argument of this book. The focus of an ethical education has continually to return to this fundamental truth, namely that for every young person in the school, both male and female, the core moral agenda of their whole lives is to become richly, deeply human; to become the full flowering of the human person that their genetic, cultural, and historical inheritance makes possible; to become a heroic player on the stage—whether large or small—of human history. Obviously, growing toward that fuller humanity also implies coming to terms with limits and the possibilities of their historical circumstances. No less obviously that implies resisting the many social and cultural structures of injustice that limit or oppress them and many others in their society. In the first chapter we reviewed some of the enormous challenges facing the human race and especially the generation currently in schools and universities. The working out of all our human destinies will involve engaging these challenges at some level.

Erikson refers to the need for societies experiencing rapid technological changes to establish and preserve flexible forms of child rearing and education that will accommodate the developmental growth of healthy children through the expected challenges of the life cycle. He sees this ongoing readjustment of child rearing and education as "a matter of human survival" (Erikson, 1980). He argues that the older generations will need to invent and support an integrated series of educational environments that correspond appropriately to the healthy development of the young toward a rich human identity. This enables us to link the themes developed in chapter two—autonomy, connectedness, and transcendence—with Erikson's mapping of the geography of human development. I emphasized in chapter two that these were foundational qualities, human dispositions toward becoming an ethically mature person.

Emphasis on those themes during the K-12 years facilitates the growth of the young persons toward moral maturity, the very maturity the adolescent begins to reach for in those transitional years toward adulthood. By sensitizing the young to the responsibilities of membership in the world, educators will have developed the common vocabulary and habits of inquiry during their years of formal schooling so as to better equip the young to move forward in their human journey, the very journey Erikson has so well illuminated.

If this agenda is "a matter of human survival," then it qualifies as a moral imperative to cultivate such a schooling process. This book takes such a moral imperative seriously. Furthermore, though a modest initial attempt, it sets out to link a flexible and integrated series of educational activities with an intentional effort to situate those major issues developed in the first chapter clearly within such activities.

PART **II**

Essentials for Cultivating
an Ethical School

CHAPTER 6

The Moral Character of Learning

Introduction

In the previous chapters we have reviewed some of the significant research and theory on the moral development of the human person. By placing the studies of the moral development of young people within the larger scheme of human development across the life span, we have been able to appreciate how the work of young people in the slow construction of a personal identity integrates the learnings of a moral order in human life into the ordering of a consistent and coherent human persona, whether male or female. Seen against the geography of life-span human development, we can understand how the overarching concern with self-development (again, differentiated by gender, but united in promoting growth of the human) during the first twenty or so years of a person's life can be seen as a pre-ethical period during which the foundation for an ethical life is constructed. During those years, engaging the developmental challenges of trust, autonomy, initiative, and industry are steps in the construction of a personal identity. That identity incorporates the acquired dispositions to trust, to own oneself and one's choices, to explore the possibilities and parameters of one's cultural and social environment, and to develop and master a variety of social, physical, cultural, and intellectual skills into a growing sense of self-confidence and self-worth that enables the choice and embrace of a journey and a future as *this* person. That choice is not made in a locked closet; rather, it is a choice made with an acquired sense of the world one lives in, deeply influenced by one's socialization, by one's class and cultural inheritance, and by the historical presuppositions and world views and social imaginaries in one's life world. With the advantages and disadvantages these influences contribute to the young person's sense of the world, and assuming a relatively healthy response to the challenges leading up to and through the formation of identity, that person is reasonably ready to step into the adult world and engage that world responsibly. That is, the person is ready for ethical engagement, for the mutuality that living an ethical life requires. In this chapter, we will explore the journey of young persons through the formal learning process during the first twelve or thirteen years of schooling, and how that learning process might be both an intellectual and a moral journey, a journey that prepares those young persons for the transition into ethical lives.

The Moral Agenda of Learners

Sometimes, perhaps most of the time, teachers forget that the youngsters in their classrooms have a rich, if complicated, life of their own. Neither the school, nor the teacher "owns" them. They are not cardboard people, zombies patiently waiting to be programmed with the official "right answers" by their teacher. Somehow the universe has patiently waited to give birth to each one of them. Each one has the right to his or her destiny, the right to fashion a life for themselves—in relationship to their community, to be sure, but as something to be *negotiated and improvised* within their community. Each of them has an intrinsic moral agenda that belongs to them as full human beings. That moral agenda is to find, create, own, and be true to themselves. It is not an agenda they can turn over to their parents, to their teachers, to the community elders, to the state. It is an agenda that tacitly unfolds for them every day of their lives, as they learn to negotiate relationships, neighborhoods, new challenges, and unexpected surprises. It is an agenda that they do not shelve or surrender when they enter the school grounds; nor do educators have the right to demand that they do so. Moreover, this is not simply the agenda of isolated individuals. It is the moral agenda of their whole generation, the agenda of all the children in the classroom, the agenda not only of creating and fashioning "me" but the agenda of creating "us." Individuals have to find out how to belong as well as how to be. Being with and belonging contains specific moral challenges which help to define the "me" an individual is discovering how to be.

What the school must do in order to activate the moral character of learning is to connect the learning agenda of the school to the central moral agenda of the learners during their thirteen or more years in school, namely, the agenda of finding and choosing and fashioning themselves as individuals and as a human community. As human beings they are searching, and must search for the truth of who they are. Educators miss this connection because they are accustomed to view the learning agenda of the school as an end in itself, rather than as a means for the moral and intellectual "filling out" of learners as human beings. Schools seem to assume that their learning agenda stands above and outside of the personal and civic life of learners. By and large the message communicated to learners is: Leave your personal and civic lives at the schoolhouse door—certainly at the classroom door—and subject yourselves to the discipline of learning the school's curriculum.

Learners, however, are full human beings. They have a life outside of the classroom, a life-world filled with family relationships, friends and enemies in the neighborhood, hobbies, and interests. They are engaged in a very important agenda of their own, namely to figure out who they are, how to make and keep friends, how the social and natural worlds make sense, and how they fit and participate in those worlds.

The Private and the Public Self

Young children gradually discover that they have an inside world and an outside world. They can conceal that inside world from adults if they choose. The inside world is the world of the running self-commentary on their experiences. It is their personal autobiography in the making. The inner world creates a silent conversation with the outer world, weighing its challenges and demands, its satisfactions and humiliations, its possibilities and its limitations. It is revealed somewhat in personal journals and diaries, but even there, the written expression is often incapable of capturing the fine nuances of feeling and impression that course throughout the inner life.

This inner life is where the child begins the journey or the quest for authenticity. That is the quest to be a genuine actor on the stage of life, rather than an indistinguishable face in the crowd, or worse, an anonymous spectator in the audience. It is a journey to becoming real, to discovering who one wants to be, who one has to be in order to fulfill one's destiny. The inner journey continuously grapples with the question of responsibility, of ownership of one's choices and actions: "Do I want to do this, or am I simply doing this to please others, or because I'm afraid to be ridiculed if I speak my mind?" While the young person seeks acceptance among peers and a modicum of respect, there is a struggle to be true to one's sense of values. The inner journey seeks consistency between outer behavior and inner convictions.

Over time, the outer journey becomes a focus of continuous exploration as one negotiates expanding relationships with parents, siblings, friends, neighbors, and school mates. That exploration involves relationships with one's cultural heritage through celebrations of weddings, birthdays, funerals, and holidays, with extended family and the family's religious community. These experiences come to be seen as consistent with or differing from the wider cultural world. Relationships with peers who are different are influenced by cultural stereotypes and negotiated (or not) through the basic rubrics of sociality. Exploration of the biophysical world of one's body, and of the natural environment and its seasonal characteristics offer tacit insights into one's relationship to the world of nature. Throughout this process of learning, the young person comes to see that learning involves something like a dialogue between the knower and the known. The learner has to listen to, question, and observe how the world of culture, nature, and society reveals itself to him or her. Sometimes it is a recognition of a pattern, sometimes it is the surprise of something unexpected, sometimes it is simply a mystery, an unanswered question of why things are the way they are: Why does the tide rise and fall? Where do clouds come from? Why do other kids tease me? Why does my team always have to lose? What is X in all these algebra problems?

Relationality as the Basis of Meaningful Learning

Learning is what happens as we understand something about why things are the way they are, or why things happen the way they do. Things are the way they are because they are in relationship to a bunch of other things. We make meaning when we can grasp what some of these relationships tell us why this something happens the way it does. The natural sciences involve the study of the relationships between things or systems in nature; those relationships help us understand how and why nature works the way it does—where clouds come from; why the ocean rises and falls; what makes lights light; where headaches come from; what diabetes does to one's body; why atomic energy is risky business. Literature is the study or expression of why humans are the way they are, what's the relationship of their feelings about themselves and how they treat other people, what is tragic and what is comic about human existence. Poetry is the expression of how people feel about some human experiences, how those experiences lead them to see how the world works, how they themselves work, how things can be metaphors for other things, how just the right word in the right place changes the music of an experience. History tries to explain why things happened they way they did, and why they keep happening in the present. History presents evidence of people making choices, making mistakes, making inventions (like the automobile) that ushered in all kinds of new relationships. Revisionist historians, in turn, provide evidence of new explanations of what happened that give different meanings to past events and different interpretations to present events.

The Moral Character of Learning and the School's Academic Curriculum

Unfortunately, much of the research on moral education deals more with out of school, or out of classroom learnings, not so much with learning as a process, but with snapshots of where youngsters are on a continuum of potential understandings of what constitutes a moral position on a dilemma or problem. Advocates of character education tend to assign an explicit curriculum for developing and sustaining character, leaving the substance of the academic curriculum as a separate matter altogether, as though achievement in academics is different from achieving character. Our approach, however, is to embrace the academic curriculum as a primary carrier of moral development toward a moral identity.

The academic curriculum of language proficiency, humanities, fine and performing arts; of the natural sciences and mathematics; of history and the social sciences—this curriculum introduces students to the worlds they already inhabit, the world of culture, the world of nature, and the world of society. These worlds already live in them; as well, these young pupils already inhabit these worlds. As cultured beings, biophysical beings, social beings, they are members of these worlds. Their membership in these worlds constitute much of their identity as humans. The academic disciplines of the school's curriculum potentially open doors into these worlds, help learners to understand how these worlds work, enable learners to find themselves in these worlds, to understand how to participate in these worlds as members.

Let us further pursue this perspective on the relationship between the moral agenda of the learner to become a somebody with value and dignity and the learning agenda of the school as represented in the academic curriculum. The school should connect the academic agenda with the learners' moral agenda in such a way that the moral activity of learning speaks to and challenges the moral agenda of the learner, and the moral agenda of learners activates and energizes the moral character of learning. In what way, then, is learning the academic curriculum a moral activity?

Learning the academic curriculum, as we are describing it here, involves the learners in exploring their identity as members of the worlds of culture, nature, and society. As members of these worlds, learners have rights and responsibilities. The more one learns about the worlds of culture, nature, and society, the more capable one becomes to participate as a responsible member of those worlds. Choosing to participate responsibly requires both knowledge and understanding, as well as a commitment to uphold the integrity, the truths (both pleasant and unpleasant) about these worlds. That is moral as well as intellectual work.

We may categorize the activity of learning as work, work that requires a level of presence to what one is working with and working on, a dialogue with the intelligibility of what one is working with and working on. That intelligibility involves mutuality, an intuition of the relationality between the worker and the subject of the work. The object of the work has its own integrity, its own authenticity. The methods the learner uses to explore that integrity and authenticity have their own built in craft discipline. The methods of studying the subject and the methods of reporting the knowledge gained, the "findings," are to be used care-fully.

That knowledge will always begin, for better or worse, as personal. The learner will approach the subject matter using past learnings and life experiences, relating the new material to the internal encyclopedia of what the learner already knows. Gradually, through classroom sharing and discussion, personal meanings become reshaped into what the group seems to agree are their public meanings. Learners talk themselves into understanding what they know. The back-and-forth between personal and public shared meanings makes the knowledge available for public use, available now for various applications to real situations in public life (Applebee, 1996). Only gradually does that knowledge begin to resemble the already catalogued and polished, abstract academic knowledge of the scholar.

The way the product of the work of the learner is assessed ought to have some relationship to the way it is produced, namely, as initially an unfinished personal meaning, and then as the product of shared understanding—an initially tentative public, social meaning. Instead, most classrooms demand that learning look like—*from the outset*—the finished work of the academic scholar. Forcing it to look like the finished product catalogued in textbooks is what contributes to make-believe learning, a learning all too quickly wrenched away from the inside dialogue between the learner and the subject in order to meet an artificial time schedule set up by the school authorities. The continuous demands for almost instantaneous conversion of the preliminary steps of learning into the finished product of the textbook (the "right answer" the teacher and the testers expect) easily convinces the learner that the school does not take the work of authentic learning at all seriously. Rather, the learner realizes that the school is set up to enforce inauthentic, make-believe learning.

The authenticity of the learner as a learner is at stake every day at school. The school either supports that authenticity or it warps and suppresses it through the routines of its pedagogy, through the very limited time and space allotted for learning, and the hurried and harrying assessment procedures employed. If the work of learning implicates the personal authenticity of the human beings involved in it as well as the integrity of the subject being studied, then young people attending schools find themselves in triple jeopardy. They can find neither themselves, nor the authentic subject being studied, nor the integrity of the learning activity itself, in what they are made to do in school.

These young learners are in the process of figuring out who they are, where and how they belong, whether they are intrinsically worthwhile, how to manage daily the confusing and ambiguous feelings about the relationships in their lives, how to defend themselves from humiliation and ridicule. At the same time they are acutely aware of how little they know about anything and how awkward and clumsy they feel when faced with the social, natural and cultural worlds that both invite and challenge them into being real as they enter into belonging relationships.

They also want to be needed, to have a sense that they have something to contribute. They want to feel competent, feel that the activity they are engaged in is something that they can master. They want some sense of being publicly involved. But that activity has to have some integrity to it, has to make sense, have some perceived connection and value for their lives. The activity they are called upon to master, demanded to master, however, is the activity of learning the curriculum of the textbook and producing its prepackaged knowledge, using the discourse of subject matter scholars to convince the teachers and the test makers that they have indeed "mastered" the curriculum.

Many studies (e.g., Applebee, 1996; Drummond, 2001; Egan, 1997; Reay & Williams, 2001; Shultz & Cook-Sather, 2001) tend to confirm that the moral agenda that young people feel, namely their obligation to become whole, to be real, to own themselves, to make their way, to say their truth, to make a contribution, to be involved in matters of public importance, to be engaged in real work, is by and large ignored, disregarded, actively rejected in many schools. Instead learners are expected to study for right answers in a curriculum that remains detached from their journey of self-definition and self-commitment.

In any community's effort to educate its children and youth through late adolescence—in the process of preparing them to participate in the ongoing life of the community as involved stewards of the common good, and as productive workers who contribute to the community's sustainable prosperity, and as sociable neighbors who share the public resources in equitable and responsible ways—the community's educative process should promote a learning process that cultivates a deep and broad understanding of the interconnectedness of humans to their natural, cultural and social environment, and that cultivates a responsibility for sustaining, correcting, and enriching those environments in their roles as citizens, neighbors, and workers.

Having hinted at the chasm between the school's learning agenda (achieving the right answers to the tests that measure the mastery of the state-defined curriculum standards) and the students' learning agenda (the existential task of becoming a somebody in the drama of everyday life with all of its ambiguities and challenges), we have to ask ourselves where schools went wrong. To understand what persistently reinforces that chasm, we have to highlight the distorted epistemology that tends to dominate schools' operational definition of learning.

The way school curriculum and classroom teaching is structured, it would seem that knowledge is understood as something an isolated learner steals or coaxes or conjures from a social, cultural, or natural world that stands at a distance over against the isolated knower.

Basic Assumptions: The Isolated Individual and the Need for Irrefutable Proof[5]

One of the most profound flaws in modernity was the gradual emergence of an aggressive assertion of the necessity for the autonomous individual. This assertion eventually developed into a philosophical, political, and economic theory and became firmly entrenched as an ideology of individualism, an unquestioned dogma that the individual, in order to be fully human, had to assert his independence from family, community, nature, God, cosmos. The individual had to stand alone against the cosmic, political, and religious landscape. To admit any intrinsic dependence on that landscape was to negate, it was believed, the individual's uniqueness, the particular destiny, the freedom to be the one-of-a-kind person all individuals were entitled to be.

That ideology had profound consequences for understanding how such an isolate individual could know the world from which the individual stood decidedly apart. It led to Descartes' struggle to build a logical basis for knowing even that he existed; his "cogito, ergo sum" (I think, therefore I am) was the act of an isolated individual who had to be the sole explanation of his own knowledge, since his standing apart from the world left him no secure bridge or connection to that world. Descartes' radically isolated knower became the starting point for most of the subsequent epistemologies of the modern world.

Somehow the mind of this isolated separated knower had to be predisposed to know the world objectively whether through innate ideas, or through logical and perceptual mechanisms whose forms naturally conformed to the logical and conceptual forms of objective realities grasped through reason and the methodologies of science. Much of cognitive science is today still wrestling with what is basically the epistemological question inherited from Descartes (Bruner, 1987).

Knowledge as Coming to Know Mutual Relationships

New understandings of knowledge and learning have emerged in the past century, which help us overcome the isolation of the knower. The new sociology of knowledge places the knower inside culture, inside an historical tapestry of already constructed knowledge and language maps, frameworks, theories, logics, and methodologies (McCarthy, 1996). The knower knows by receiving the culture's knowledge already constructed for the knower by the community that enfolds the knower. That prior knowledge, of course, did not fall from the sky. It was constructed by humans already conditioned by their accepted frameworks and methodologies of their time. The construction of new knowledge, however, always had to struggle against the accepted frameworks and methodologies, for they defined the status quo and therefore occupied a privileged position in society as well as in the academy. Knowledge in any society is always in the process of being constructed, deconstructed, and reconstructed because of changing circumstances, new technologies, new power relationships in society. Knowledge generation is therefore a social and a political process, contested, creative, adaptive, exploratory—a journey of collective human intelligences, sometimes collaborating, sometimes competing for clarity and depth of understanding as well as for public legitimacy and political advantage.

If knowledge is not a particular something that an isolated individual somehow steals or coaxes or conjures from a hostile or indifferent nature, then what is it? To overcome the riddle of knowledge, we must overturn one of the basic assumptions that have led to the riddle in the first place, and that is the assumption of an isolated knower, separated from the natural, social, and cultural worlds he or she is trying to know. More recently, philosophers and scientists have come to view the human and natural worlds as defined, not by physical or social atomism, but by relationality. Dewey, Whitehead, Polanyi, Bateson and many others suggest that we begin with the assumption that the individual human being is not isolated from nature or society but is in a dynamic relationship of mutuality to all of nature as well as to the social and cultural worlds. Being in relationship to the natural, social, and cultural worlds means being in multiple relationships simultaneously: relationships to, for example, gravity, the food chain, weather patterns, one's family history, to the Japanese stock market, the Australian wool market, the Middle East oil market, clothing designers, technological inventions, one's children and their children. Knowledge is what emerges from the intentional exploration of those relationships, whether those relationships are benign or problematic.

Knowledge is a dialogue between the intelligences found in the natural, cultural, and social worlds and the intelligences of individual knowers. Being in relationship with the natural, cultural, and social worlds implies mutual involvement and mutual respect. It implies a language or languages by which a dialogue takes place. The knower and the known speak to one another, resist one another, attract one another, threaten one another, seduce one another, puzzle one another. Since they naturally belong to one another, since they exist continuously in relationship to one another, there is no question of the knower living independently on some higher plane above the known. They are intertwined, implicated in each other's existence. This holds for relationships of love and relationships of enmity; relationships between humans and songbirds, and humans and the HIV virus; relationships between spouses and relationships between jailers and prison inmates, relationships with weeds in my backyard and with irruptions on the sun's surface. Unless the experiences of these relationships issue in a dialogue of mutual understanding at some minimal level, then there is no knowledge—perhaps information or data, but little or no knowledge.

Knowledge as Familiarity and Respect Leading to Responsibility

Knowledge, in other words, can be understood from the standpoint of *relationality*, from an ontology, not of isolated beings, but of beings in a field, the energy of which grounds, creates, and sustains relationality. Looked at this way, we may speak of knowledge as the achievement of a certain mutual familiarity or intimacy.

If we postulate that knowing is somewhat like loving, the approach to the object of knowledge requires a profound respect for and sensitivity to its integrity. Authentic knowing slowly reveals the relationship between the knower and the known. Authentic knowing gradually implies responding dialogically to the intelligibility of the known as the known can be interpreted in human categories. From this perspective, knowing is not only a meeting between intelligences, it is also an implicit moral act. In that moral act of knowing, the knower accepts the responsibility of coming to know the known carefully—that is, full of care for the integrity of the known. That implies avoiding a careless approach or superior attitude to the dialogue, so that the knower knows the known as it truly is, or at least as truly as present circumstances allow.

Sometimes knowledge is seen as a process of gaining power over the object of knowledge, or as something to be used for self-promoting purposes. That is to miss the point of the knowing process. Coming to know generates an affirming and enabling power of entering more fully into communion with the world, of sharing in the depth, richness, and struggles of the world, of becoming a richer, deeper, stronger human being who is more firmly rooted in the depth and soul of the world. Learning, then, means putting aside one's own sense of superiority or importance, leaving one's own self-centered agenda aside, submitting oneself to the message of the subject, letting the subject re-position the self in a new or clearer set of relationships (natural, social, cultural), allowing the self to be humbled by the complexity of the known. It also means that the knower, when she or he shares their knowledge of the known, represents the known as accurately and as sensitively as circumstances allow.

The Social Responsibility of Knowledge Utilization

Beside the knowledge of the other as it is in itself and in relationship to the knower, knowledge also reveals the relationships between the properties of various things. One knows the properties of types of steel, types of gasses, types of acids. One knows that certain gasses when heated will melt steel; that certain acids will corrode steel. One knows that steel is "stronger" than wood, and that a steel axe can cut through wood. One knows that termites can eat wood. One discovers that certain microbes will help to diffuse an oil spill, and that a certain circumference of pipe will allow only a certain volume of water to flow through it at any time. Rarely, however, are these isolated, one-to-one relationships. For example, water will flow through pipes according to conditions of pressure, as well as conditions of gravity; water will not flow through a pipe going up a hill unless it is pumped, or unless the water source is already at a height above the hill. Microbes cannot be introduced into a water system to dispel an oil spill unless the water is sufficiently warm to sustain the life and activity of the microbes. The knowledge that one acquires not only reveals the relationships the knower has to the world, but it also reveals how the world works, or how, with some inventiveness, one can make it work. Knowledge not only teaches reverence for the world, it reveals the actual or potential working relationships of the world.

Knowledge is useful for one's work in the world. That work involves not only a career; it involves one's work as a member of a family, as a neighbor, as a citizen, as a homebuilder, as a member of multiple organizations, as a member of the human race, as an intelligent animal in the natural environment. Often one's work is indeed focused on one's career. That is where many make their public contribution to the world. That work involves intelligence, artistry, energy. It also involves a basic sense of obligation, obligation not simply to one's employer to give an honest day's work for a day's pay, but an obligation to the world—however amorphous our definition of that term might be—to make a contribution, to respond to some minimal sense of stewardship.

There are, unfortunately, many examples of unscrupulous people who use their knowledge in exclusively self-serving ways. Almost every day the media carry reports of people and companies violating the trust of their profession or their craft: insider trading, tax fraud, bribery of public officials, shoddy field testing of medicines, misleading manipulation of experimental research results, cost-cutting procedures that endanger the lives of automobile drivers, violations of health code regulations in food-processing plants, insurance companies that refuse to honor the terms of their policies, violations of construction safety codes, willful violations of workers' workplace safety regulations.

The public is outraged precisely because of the public trust in the integrity of professionals. Their position of superior knowledge and expertise leads us to place significant aspects of our lives in their hands (Sokolowski, 1991). Their crimes are more serious than that of crimes of passion, the fight in the tavern, the drug-crazed street robber. The professional violates the public's respect for their role as public servant when they use their profession to break the law and to defraud the customer. The unfortunate cynicism toward lawyers and doctors, business executives and politicians, teachers and clergy is not only a measure of the public's disappointment at their behavior; it is also a measure of the continued high expectations of the moral ideal of their professions.

Two Teachers With Different Understandings of Learning

Think now of how knowledge is approached in schools. Imagine two different kinds of teachers. Let us call one teacher Stan and the other Connie. Stan assumes that knowledge is objectively out there awaiting a knower, assumes that the student is independent and separated from what he knows, assumes that learning is simply a matter of appropriating that knowledge, either by memorization of its formulation in the textbook, or by performing lab experiments that will lead to the development of correct research skills and to answers already prescribed in the textbook. Knowledge is a question of getting and knowing how to get the right answers. The right answers are what the experts know and have told us is what we need to know about the matter. The process of explaining what lies behind the "right answer" is almost always neglected in Stan's classes.

Covering the syllabus is equated with mastering the objective knowledge contained in the state curriculum standards. Depending on how many right and wrong answers a student comes up with in the course of a semester, a student receives a grade, indicating "how much" of the syllabus he has learned, how much he knows.

When students takes the high stakes test, their "achievement" is expressed in the number of right answers achieved on the test. Stan explains to his class that they are involved in a high stakes process. They have to prepare for a state exam which will determine whether they are promoted or held back. Success in the state exam will mean that they have what it takes to be productive citizens in future endeavors. If they work hard, stay focused, work at the daily assignments and correct their mistakes as soon as they are aware of them, if they stay up with the flow of the course, they will be successful. In order to help them prepare for the state exams he will provide them with many exercises that pose questions similar to the ones they'll have on the exam. They'll have a chance to practice answering questions like the ones on the test.

Stan's weekly lesson plans are carefully matched to the state curriculum standards for the academic level of his students. He provides drills, spot quizzes, team competitions throughout the week to make sure students have sufficient time-on-task learning the material contained in the curriculum standards. His students practice test-taking skills as well, learning how to narrow down the possible responses to multiple choice questions, and how to construct a preliminary outline for an essay-type response on the test.

Connie's classroom teaching reflects an enthusiastic fascination with the material being studied. Learners sense that she actually enjoys "messing around with this stuff." She communicates such enthusiasm for the material under study that even normally resistant ones will go along so as not to hurt her feelings. Connie invites her learners to enter the world of the subject matter, whether that is chemistry, mathematics, or poetry. Entry into that world, however, is not as a tourist; rather, they enter into a world where they are dramatically implicated, where they are in relationship with what they are learning, where they become responsible for and to what they know.

Connie also advises her learners about the process involved in preparing for the high stakes state exams. She points out, however, that the curriculum standards, while helpful in highlighting important and interesting things to learn, represent an artificial construction of a sequence of learnings that, in being divided into separate curriculum strands, tend to conceal the many relationships between the strands of knowledge. She spends time preparing for the high stakes tests, but within a context of learning as an exciting and soul-expanding journey. Her weekly lesson plans have one eye on the curriculum standards and another eye on creating a dialogue with the subject matter, seeking to stimulate a fascination with the intelligence embedded in whatever they are studying. By encouraging a dialogue between their intelligence and the intelligence in the realities they are studying, she is helping her learners engage the methodologies needed to carry on the dialogue, methodologies of measurement, observation, imaginative exploration of alternative scenarios, seeking for evidence of various types of relationships, uncovering the logic behind a relationship.

Connie knows that that kind of dialogue between intelligences is the way that knowledge is constructed. She also realizes that learners are constructed by knowledge, even as they construct knowledge. Assuming that knowledge is grounded in relationality, then knowledge will reveal how the knower is in relationship to the known. Learning about chemical compounds not only illuminates the ecology of the immediate environment, but also reveals how their own body works. Learning about World War II re-places them in relationship to their own willingness to die for their country, in relationship to non-violence as a desirable ethic, in relationship to weapons of mass destruction, in relationship to the actual sufferings of civilian populations, in relationship to the reality of genocide, in relationship to political fanaticism, in relation to the geopolitics of current history. Connie encourages her learners both to take responsibility for what they know and to be responsible to what they know.

Learning for right answers is replaced with learning how to live in some kind of harmony with their natural and social world. There is no one right answer to that larger agenda. The knowledge learners absorb, however, continues to illuminate their relationship to their natural and social world, relationships that continue to become more intelligible, and relationships that make demands on them and demands on their generation. Connie also provides them with experiences in the use of their knowledge to analyze and respond to problems in the real world. For example, through computer simulations, she sets her learners to work on an engineering problem, on an investment strategy, on a census taking issue. Again, using case studies and computer simulations, she presents them with problems from the world of public health, environmental protection, food-processing technologies, and genetic research.

In social studies Connie has them construct family histories using stories from relatives still alive, letters from deceased relatives, old newspaper stories, family picture albums. She requires them not only trace their genealogies, but also to attempt to understand the human and civil rights issues their forebears faced, the technologies available to them for various survival tasks, their cultural enjoyments and artifacts.

In the process of learning the curriculum standards, Connie teaches her learners how to use their knowledge, how to apply what they know to real people and real situations. In the process she teaches them how to honor the tools of generating knowledge and applying knowledge, how to report their findings with integrity; how to avoid going beyond the evidence and to announce speculation when it is being employed. Furthermore, she requires them to apply their knowledge and imagination to explore ways to improve the situation under study. How might the public health department better monitor the processing of food or the levels of bacteria in the water supply? How might companies change their policies toward whistle-blowers to encourage early detection of serious production problems? How might human rights abuses in developing countries be more effectively treated in international law? Connie encourages her learners to use their knowledge in the service of people in the local community. She has them reflect how it feels to use their knowledge as a service to others, rather than simply as a means to getting a grade on a test. In this way, they learn an important life-long lesson: that their talents were given to them primarily to serve the community.

The practice of using and applying their knowledge will be accompanied by a continuous stream of admonitions such as: Knowledge brings responsibility; if we do not use our knowledge to improve people's lives, to contribute to the human journey, then what good is it? Respect the integrity of what you know and how you came to know it. Respect the craft of language and rhetoric. Respect the audience who receives your knowledge reports by providing them illustrative examples and precise language and occasional humor for when they get drowsy.

Echoing the wisdom of Whitehead (1957), her major sermon to her learners is this: "You do not have the moral option to choose not to learn. Choosing not to learn is choosing not to know who you are and what you will need to know in order to make a contribution to the world. Your chosen ignorance may lead to self-deception, to the shrinking of the horizon of your possibilities. Your chosen ignorance may be the occasion of an accident, the loss of life, the failure of an important project, the frustration of a community's dream, the disappointment of people who were counting on you to perform. An organization's or a community's achievement of excellence is dependent not only on the quality of its most talented members, but upon the intelligent cooperation of people like you and me. The shoddy or incompetent work of anyone diminishes the achievement of the whole.

"We have achieved as a civilization whatever level of greatness, whatever level of excellence, whatever level of good order because countless people like you and me knew what to do when it counted most. They were prepared. That's why learning what you learn in school is not only a privilege, it is a duty to yourselves and to your community and to your future children and grandchildren."

Summary and Conclusion

Thus far we have been exploring the meaning of the moral nature of human learning. The moral agenda of the learner, namely to become a somebody, a real person, and then to participate authentically in the "us" that engages in self-governance and community, of necessity involves coming into an authentic relationship to other humans and to the natural, social, and cultural worlds that the learner inhabits with other humans. Establishing those authentic relationships with the natural, social, and cultural worlds not only plays an essential part in the self-understanding and the self-construction of the learner, but also points to the multiple responsibilities that all the learners have to those worlds and for those worlds. This is real learning. The other kind of learning that goes on in school seems artificial, superficial, fake, phony, make believe, and therefore untruthful. In many, if not most schools, this form of fake learning is the unspoken norm that is both supported and rewarded. Cultivating an ethical school challenges those norms and offers alternatives that support authentic learning.

CHAPTER 7

The Ethics of Teaching

This chapter attempts to clarify the distinction between what is sometimes called "General Ethics" and "Professional Ethics," specifically in the field of education. With that distinction clarified, the chapter then pursues what the particular "good" is that the profession of teaching uniquely cultivates. The elaboration of the moral goodness of learning and, by association, teaching, begins to clarify the deepest value dimensions of the profession of teaching and provides a platform for educational leaders to argue for and sustain its integrity. Needless to say, the preceding chapter already has pointed the way toward these value dimensions of the practice of teaching.

Delineating the Professional Ethics of Teaching

General ethics in education is more concerned with the ethics of everyday life as that gets played out in the institutional context of schools and involves issues around fairness, truth telling, respect, equity, conflict, misunderstandings, and loyalties. Most case studies in the literature on ethics in teaching, or in educational administration (Strike, Haller, & Soltis, 1998; Zaretsky, 2005; Langlois & Lapointe, 2004) deal with ethics in education from this position. Professional ethics has much more to do with the ethics of the profession of educating. Part of that special ethics is about preventing harm in the process of educating; but part of that ethics is about promoting the good involved in the practice of educating (Shapiro & Stefkovich, 2001).

Just as medical ethics is concerned with promoting the good of its professional practice, which is physical health; just as business ethics is supposed to be concerned with promoting the public and individual good involved in trade, commerce, and contracts, just so one would expect educational ethics to be grounded in the particular good involved in teaching and learning. What is that good that education is supposed to pursue, promote, support? Shapiro and Stefkovich (2001) advance that that particular good is "the best interests of the child." I want to specify that in schools, the best interests of the child is the good to be found in learning—not any old kind of learning, but in a deep and broad learning that enables the child to accelerate the process of self-understanding and agency in relation to the natural, the cultural, and the social worlds. The good of learning involves the good of discovering, naming, constructing oneself as one is introduced to the natural, cultural and social worlds that constitute one's public "situatedness." The good of learning involves, as well, learning to enact one's life as an agent as least as much as a patient, that is, to participate as a member of those worlds. The ethics of teaching then comes to focus very intentionally on the *proactive* pursuit, cultivation, and support of those goods of learning in and for a democratic community and polity.

The current scholarship on ethics in education has done a reasonably good job of describing the general ethics of teaching in and administering schools but not a good enough job of describing what the proactive pursuit of those *special goods of learning* might look like. Lacking that clearer focus on the proactive pursuit of those goods of learning, the profession of teaching fails to grasp that their core work—not the work that surrounds that core work like communicating with parents, avoiding racism or religious prejudice in the classroom, collaboratively setting up the ground-rules that will govern classroom behavior, but the core work of the complex and intricate craft of teaching—is moral work. The general ethics of justice, care, and critique (Starratt, 1991, chapter two of this book) provide guidance for how to respond to students, colleagues, parents, policy makers, and the public at large ethically while going about the core work of their profession. General ethics, however, do not provide sufficient ethical insight into the specialized professional work of teaching, a work whose moral character is intimately tied into cultivating the moral character of learning.

The Ethics of Teaching Is Bound Up with the Ethics of Learning

Teaching is the practice of a profession; that profession professes to stimulate and cultivate and sustain learning in its deep and broad sense

(Hargreaves & Fink, 2006; Nixon et al., 1996; Sizer, 1996; Wood, 1998). As Macintyre observes,

> What is distinctive of a practice is in part the way in which conceptions of the relevant goods and ends which the technical skills serve—and every practice does require the exercise of technical skills—are transformed and enriched by these extensions of human powers and by that regard for its own internal goods which are partially definitive of each particular practice or type of practice. (1981, p. 180)

The good of learning, then, can be asserted as the good which the technical skills of teaching serve and which are transformed and enriched by the extension of human powers which learning produces.

The activity of learning, however, is itself a large generalization. What is the special good of the learning that takes place in schools, a good so important that societies everywhere throughout history have attended to its preservation? It is the good of learning, in an organized way (frequently referred to as the scope and sequence of the curriculum) the accumulated wisdom of the tribe or nation about how the world of nature works, how the social world works, how the cultural/religious world works. That learning involves learning about who one is by how one belongs to the biophysical, social, cultural, and religious worlds, about the rights and responsibilities of membership in these worlds. In societies that separate religion from the education of the young in secular subjects, religious education is left to families and those religious communities they belong to. School learnings constitute such an important good for both the individual young person, the community of young persons, and the adult society, that they are usually placed under the direction of persons who have made a special effort to systematize, or organize that knowledge in its basic intelligibility, who, in short, practice the profession of education. The assumption behind this formalized process of teaching and learning is that through it, the new generation of members will be able to participate as full adults in carrying on and renewing the life of the community.

The heart and soul of the ethics of teaching is to be found in the cultivation of learning in pupils. The word cultivation involves a metaphor taken from the work of agri-culture. It suggests that the teacher is somewhat like the gardener who aerates the soil, provides supports for the shrubs and plants to hold on to, prunes them, waters them and weeds the soil around them. The metaphor also implies that it is the plant that does the real work, namely the growing. The gardener supports and encourages that work, but the plant does the growing. Teaching does not do the work of learning; the student does that work. The metaphor suggests as well that the teacher is a culturing resource and model, providing critical appraisal of the learners' work the way cultural critics would, relating the students' work to criteria of style and grace, logic and clarity, robustness and sophistication, simplicity and integrity.

When we speak of teaching as cultivating learning, we also mean engaging something larger than skills and information. We mean that teaching cultivates literacy, cultivates character, cultivates taste, cultivates civic dispositions; cultivates generous understandings of the processes and patterns in nature, in social life, in cultural life; cultivates ideals, cultivates a sense of community, cultivates responsibilities.

Knowledge as Independent, Dependent, and Interior

Tom Sergiovanni (2001) suggests helpful distinctions between assumptions about knowledge. He suggests that some teachers think about *knowledge as standing above the learner*; some think of the *learner as standing above the knowledge*; still others think of *knowledge as something inside the learner*. When we think of the content knowledge of the curriculum the teacher is supposed to know, we can view it from each of those assumptions and see the implications for their professional development that flow from each assumption.

Content knowledge, for example, about Shakespeare or about genetic biology can be thought of as something standing above the teacher. It is knowledge "out there"; it is knowledge standing on its own, in books, in libraries, in the research findings of scholars. The job of the teacher is to absorb it as it is, with its scientific or aesthetic conceptual apparatus, its definitions, its research methodology, its canonical grammar, so to speak. Once the teacher has absorbed, mastered, accumulated all this objective content knowledge, the teacher shapes this knowledge into a digestible and manageable logic called the school curriculum (or has this done by a textbook publisher) for the learners to master, absorb, accumulate. The students' expression of that mastery is revealed in the students' ability to get the right answers on the test, which supposedly reflect that content area as it is "out there," uncontaminated by students' subjective interpretations and cultural applications. We see this somewhat reflected in the "Teaching for Understanding Curriculum" (Wiske, 1998), with its categories of dimensions of understanding (knowledge, method, purpose, and forms) and levels of understanding (naïve, novice, apprentice, and master) implying the gradual mastery of an academic discipline.

For others, content knowledge still remains outside the learner, standing on its own, a true reflection of some aspect of reality. The teacher, however, as the professional educator, stands above this knowledge and decides to use it in a variety of ways, sometimes in a cross disciplinary lesson ("King Henry and the Working Class," "Shakespeare's Sense of Science"), sometimes in a thematically organized unit ("Patriotism in Shakespeare, in Rupert Brooke, in Margaret Thatcher") and sometimes as a stand-alone lesson ("An analysis of the *Merchant of Venice*"). The teacher as the professional educator knows which pieces to pick and choose for certain grade levels: DNA in dinosaurs for second graders, in insects for fifth graders, in microbes for tenth graders. Learners will follow the same approach to these content areas of biology: definitions, methodology for studying genetics, identification of genetic reproductive patterns, evolutionary genetic variations, and so forth, but in more simplified form for the earlier years.

The third assumption about content knowledge is that though the content knowledge might be stimulated from the canon-ized knowledge "out there," it doesn't remain out there. It becomes the learner's knowledge; it enters into the learner's understanding of her or himself; it situates the learner in the natural, cultural, or social world, it is inside the learner; it becomes a part of her. The learner may continue to feed and enrich that inside knowledge with further study of other knowledge sources. These learners see themselves inside the realities being studied, and see these realities inside themselves. There is a dialogue between the knower and the known. The intelligibility of the known enhances the intelligibility of the knower. In naming the known, the knower is implicated in a relationship of responsibility to the known, a responsibility to name it truly, accurately, in its clear, at least for the moment, meaning. But that meaning does not stand totally outside the knower. The meaning of the known is also *what it means to me*, not in a whimsical, arbitrary way, but in a way that implicates me in the relationship to the known and in the integrity of announcing what it means to me. Thus, the knowledge gained through the learning process is *necessarily* personal, at least *partly* subjective, while at the same time capable of being presented in its public sense.

From this third perspective—and this is the perspective on learning that ties it to the intrinsically moral character of learning—everything within the biophysical, the cultural, the social worlds has within it some form of intelligence, whether that is found in its genetic or cellular intelligence, the intelligence of a human artifact, the intelligible patterns of human association. That intelligibility may have been discovered by someone else and enunciated in a theory, an interpretation, a formula. Nevertheless, in coming to know some aspect of reality, the knower has to come to know that reality in some kind of personal appropriation of that reality's intelligibility. Otherwise, all the knower would know is the formula, the theory in its verbal or mathematical expression, but not apprehend the reality those expressions pointed to. The knowledge would be of the name, but not of the reality behind the name. Without that dialogue with reality, mediated through language, theoretical frameworks, or formulae, then the intelligibility of that reality does not engage the intelligibility of the knower, for it does not illuminate any relationship with the knower's reality. The knower needs to understand that relationship if the knowledge is to mean something to the knower. Otherwise, what is the point of learning anything?

What we have said about the learner taking knowledge inside of him or herself in a dialogue between intelligences applies equally to the teacher who, before becoming a teacher, has to go through the same process of learning. Thus, "Shakespeare" is not only a corpus of poems and plays that sits on a library shelf, a body of work the teacher has read, memorized, analyzed, critiqued, perhaps even played a part in a production of. Shakespeare is now inside the teacher. Romeo, Lear, Falstaff, Richard, Hamlet, Ophelia, Cleopatra, Lady Macbeth have entered the teacher's soul, have set up a dialogue with her identity, have opened doors to the intimate chambers of the human heart and the human beast. Those characters speak to the heroic, as well as to the devious, defensive, and silly impulses of human beings. Through these characters the teacher recognizes aspects of him or herself. He also recognizes how many of these dramatic characters have become stereotypes for recognizing and naming those traits in others. They stand for the breadth and depth of human possibility, as well as for the tragic predicaments humans face.

When that teacher teaches the "content knowledge" of Shakespeare, that content knowledge can now emerge in its transformative power. Teaching Shakespeare now becomes an opportunity to help Shakespeare speak to the humanity of the learners, and thereby increase their self-knowledge and their knowledge of the heroic, the foolish, and the darker side of human nature.

Similarly, for the biology teacher, the content knowledge of genetics works its way inside. It helps the teacher understand her/himself more profoundly as a living organism in nature. A personal appropriation of genetic biology establishes a dialogue between the intelligibility of the double helix and the intelligibility of the teacher's biological inheritance. That dialogue also reveals how science enables nature to understand itself, and enables humans to understand the "mind of nature" (Augros & Stanciu, 1987; Bateson, 1979a; Eiseley, 1962; Prigogine & Stengers, 1984; Zohar & Marshall, 1994). Such knowledge places the knower in a new relationship to the worm that contains most of the genetic material that humans possess. Such knowledge places the knower in touch with an enormous history, an "immense journey" (Eiseley, 1957), of terrestrial life which has creatively and patiently struggled through day after day after day, year after year after year, century after century after century, millennium after millennium after millennium until it had finally figured out how to think for itself, then think about itself, then think about its thinking, and, finally, think about what it wanted to do with itself (Seilstad, 1989). This knowledge reveals the knower to him/herself in a profoundly transformative way.

This kind of personalized knowledge of genetic biology—attained only after considerable study and reflection—now prepares the teacher to facilitate at least the beginning of a dialogue between DNA and the learner's mind, imagination and soul. This dialogue will lead to multiple additional dialogues with DNA in worms, insects, flowers canaries, gerbils, sheep dogs, classmates, even Shakespeare and his circus parade of heroes and heroines, villains, knaves, and fools. Perhaps the English and the biology teacher might hold a seminar on the Shakespearean variations of DNA.

One might imagine that these three approaches to curriculum knowledge might reflect a progression from the first-year teacher, to the post-tenure teacher, to the mature teacher. In some teachers' development that may be the pattern. Yet, others may begin with the more mature fascination with knowledge of the world and of themselves that their discipline provides. Even these kind of beginners, however, will need to deepen their understanding of their discipline as well as broaden their pedagogical repertory to facilitate a captivating dialogue with that world for all of their students.

The cultivation of this kind of learning lies at the heart of the teacher's professional work. It is the special good which the practice of teaching promotes. In learning about the worlds of culture, society, and nature, the learner is learning what membership in those worlds means and how his or her own best interests bisect with those memberships. This analysis of learning may be brought to a larger synthesis by referring to the types of learning enunciated by the committee that formulated the vision of learning needed by all citizens in a global society (Delors et al., 1996).

In their report to the United Nations Educational, Scientific, and Cultural Organization (UNESCO), the authors foresaw that learning conceived as building a storehouse of static knowledge would not prepare the young for all the changes, challenges, and opportunities of the Twenty-first Century interdependent world. They proposed, rather, a larger view of continuous learning which schools should attend to: Learning to know; learning to do; learning to be; and learning to live together. To this vision of learning, Hargreaves and Fink (2006) add a fifth: Learning to live sustainably. The school's curriculum should stimulate these five kinds of learning as it exposes learners to the natural, cultural and social worlds in which they are assuming membership. As they learn how to learn, how to do, how to be, how to live together, how to live sustainably in the three worlds of nature, culture, and society, they will be taking inside themselves the lessons those worlds teach, creating a dialogue out of which they will continue to construct themselves as bio-physical persons, as cultural persons, as social persons. Thus will the learning process be transformative as it "extends the reach of human capabilities" (Macintyre, 1981) to embrace and enact those goods found in the learning process.

As teachers attempt to engage learners in this deep and broad kind of learning, we can see how their practice calls them to model the very kinds of learning that they hold out for their students. In the process of teaching, teachers have to learn and model how to learn, how to do, how to be, how to live together, and how to live sustainably

A Model of the Ethical Practice of Teaching

The following model attempts to capture the intrinsically moral character of teaching and learning, and, in the process to illuminate the practice of teaching at its best, as virtuous practice. The model presumes that learning is dialogical as the previous chapter and the above commentary was intended to demonstrate. The model assumes that teaching is also dialogical. Teaching flows from the teacher's dialogue with the curriculum material, and also from the teacher's dialogue with the learner before, during, and after the learning episode. With knowledge of both the students and the particular curriculum unit actively present in the teacher's mind and imagination, the teacher constructs a variety of learning activities that will bring the students into lively conversation with a piece of the curriculum unit. The model is illustrated in Figure 7.1.

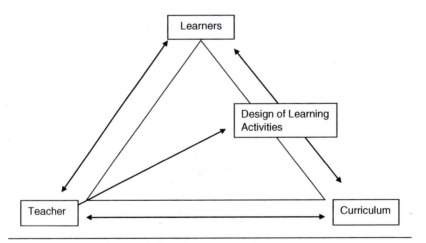

Figure 7.1 Model of relationships within the ethics of teaching.

The first order of business in a teaching learning situation is for the teacher to establish a working relationship with the learners. That relationship has first to build up some trust between the teacher and the learners. The learners need to know that the teacher is interested in them, cares for and respects them as human beings with huge potentials. The learners need to see the teacher as an authentic person, not as some distant, cardboard authority figure, but someone who can laugh and cry, someone who is consistent and reliable, someone who tells the truth.

The teacher has to try to get to know the learners as well as possible. Figure 7.2 attempts to outline the knowledge that results from that dialogue with the learners. That dialogue helps teachers know the learners' individual interests, hobbies, career interests, academic strengths and shortcomings, fears and uncertainties, family background and home context. At the start of the school year, the teachers should assess each student's readiness for the work expected of them: their reading levels, their study skills, their social skills, their cultural background and how that can

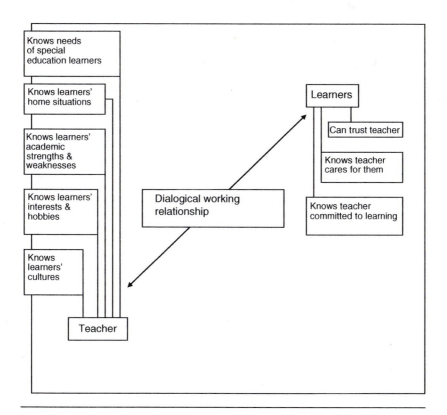

Figure 7.2 First leg of the model: Teacher's working relationship with learners.

be called upon in various learning assignments. This knowledge enables the teacher to differentiate her instruction to target the interests, talents, and deficiencies of various students in the class.

The task has grown more demanding in the last twenty-five years or so as schools have mainstreamed students with handicapping conditions ranging from physical disabilities such as blindness or deafness, to mental disabilities such as Down's syndrome, to learning difficulties such as dyslexia or attention deficit disorder, to emotional disabilities. With students identified with special learning needs, teachers have to be much more attentive and knowledgeable as they seek to uncover the ways students may effectively engage the curriculum. In many schools, teachers will be assisted by special education teachers and teacher aides who can work as a team to design appropriate learning activities more suited to particular students' abilities.

For the primary school teachers establishing a dialogue with the learners in the class is a relatively manageable task. For secondary and middle school teachers who normally teach one discipline in many classrooms during the day, getting to know over one hundred students very well is a daunting task. Some schools try to lessen the burden by having two or three teachers from the different subject areas teach the same learners for two or three successive years. That extended time frame enables those teachers to share their knowledge of that group of students and to share ideas on how to capture their interest in the curriculum and to overcome learning prob-

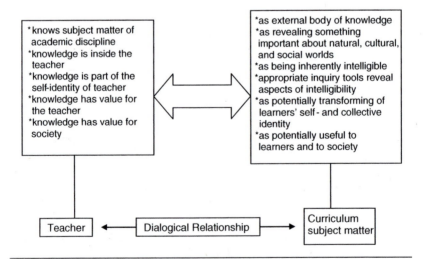

Figure 7.3 Second leg of the model: Teacher's dialogical relationship with curriculum subject matter.

lems they might be having in several subject areas. That arrangement also provides opportunities for cross-disciplinary learning activities as well as for student peer coaching.

The second leg of the triangle concerns the teacher's knowledge of the curriculum. As indicated earlier, that knowledge can be relatively superficial and naïve, as simply external knowledge of an academic area to be mastered and reproduced for assessment exercises, or it can be personalized knowledge that continues to reveal the knower's relationship to the natural, cultural, or social world. Primary teachers have a life-long agenda here, for they may know one or two academic areas reasonably well, but have a very limited mastery of several others. They have to continually listen to the curriculum content talk back to them, to show a side of its intelligibility that will be useful for students to discover, that will in turn talk back to the students and help them see more deeply how they are connected to the natural, cultural, and social worlds.

One of the challenges for primary teachers is to translate their adult understanding of the subject matter into the design of learning activities that can appeal to the minds and imaginations and feelings of their young learners, while at the same time being true to the integrity of their own understandings. This translation of the teachers' understandings of their subject matter into appealing and clarifying learning activities is, of course, a challenge for teachers at all levels. Again, because of the diversity within classrooms, much of this translation will have to be more and more customized to fit various groups of learners. Here is where the five kinds of learning mentioned above (learning to know, to do, to be, to live together, to live sustainably) may provide an enlarged imaginative landscape for the teacher to construct a variety of learning activities.

The teacher's dialogue with the curriculum will always take place with the students standing in the picture, with the teacher asking of the subject matter, "What do you have to say to these learners that might be of particular importance to their lives? How do you connect to them? How might they connect to you? How do you help them understand something about themselves that adds value to who they are? How do you re-place, re-mind these learners within the natural, cultural or social worlds?"

These questions lead naturally to the third leg of the triangle, the dialogue between the students and the subject matter. The teacher's work on this leg of the triangle involves her bringing together her knowledge of the students with her knowledge of the curriculum and designing learning activities that bring the students into active dialogue with the subject matter. Those activities can involve games, puzzles, memory tricks, projects, problems, reading and writing exercises, dramatic performances, story-telling, dance, experiments with color, shape, sounds, movements, measurement exercises, songs, debates, jigsaw exercises—whatever will bring the learners into some kind of experience with the subject matter. As the learners becomes more familiar and more comfortable with the subject matter, the teacher will inevitably involve the learners in reflective questions about how they are making sense of the material, and how the material is talking back to them.

The important part of any pedagogical scheme is to bring the knowledge from outside to inside the learner. The teacher should insist on the learner being responsible to the knowledge they are personally appropriating and constructing. That means naming what they know carefully and truthfully, not attempting to inflate their knowledge beyond what it is, not making believe that they know something when they don't. The learners should constantly be encouraged to name what they know as far as they know it, even if that knowledge is expressed tentatively, in a hunch or a guess. Such responses as "It seems to me that this story is about making friends, about the risk of making a friend, because when you tell stuff to your friend that you wouldn't tell to anyone else because they might think you're weird, you hope your friend will still accept you." The response

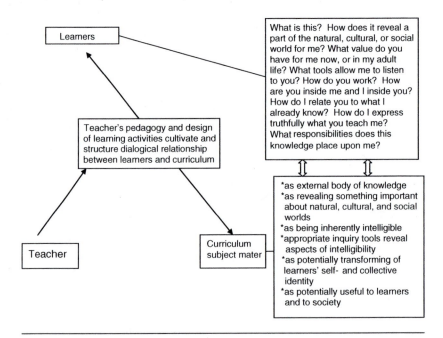

Figure 7.4 The third leg of the model: Teacher's efficacious pedagogy brings learners into dialogue with the curriculum.

indicates a learner attempting to articulate some truth about the nature of friendship, especially as the learner may have experienced it in her or his own life. The teacher might follow up with the question: "And when a friend accepts what you tell about your self as ok, how does that make you feel?" The question invites the student to generate additional learnings about friendship, not from a book, but from a dialogue with his own experience of friendship. But the teacher can also refer back to the story and ask whether the story provides confirming evidence that friendship is risky but worth the risk. The question requires the student to take elements of the story further inside to probe what his answer will be.

No matter what the academic subject matter, the teacher can always encourage this movement from outside knowledge to inside knowledge, bringing the learner into dialogue with that knowledge and how that knowledge might be in relationship to the learner, what that knowledge helps the learner to understand about her or himself or about the world in which they exercise their membership. This kind of learning process always intentionally raises the questions, "What's the point of learning this stuff? What does it have to do with us? Why is it important? What is its value for us?" Requiring the learners to answer those questions as truthfully as they can occasions that ongoing dialogue with knowledge that makes it personally significant. The teacher, however, will not necessarily require these dialogues between the learner and the subject matter every day, because sometimes the focus of the lesson will be relatively narrow or it may not lend itself to that kind of reflective learning. Often, such deep, internalizing of the learning is more appropriate toward the end of a larger unit of the curriculum.

Implications of the Model for Teachers' Growth

Teachers will always be refining their pedagogical skills and strategies. One of the obvious reasons behind professional development programs is precisely to support improvement of their pedagogical skills and strategies. Often these programs, however, provide a kind of cookbook menu of exercises, a new bag of tricks to hook students into learning the material, without being grounded in any kind of deeper purpose than it helps learners prepare for exams. What this third leg of the triangle provides is that deeper rationale to the learning process which should guide and shape all of the pedagogical skills and strategies the teacher employs.

Let us listen to a teacher's reflection on her individually devised professional development project to target her pedagogy towards the perceived needs of students.

> The most beneficial aspect of the process was probably the initial planning of it...thinking about it even before the implementing... thinking in my own mind what I could do with my particular group of students and my unique situation...what would be one thing that I could really work on and concentrate on this year that would impact them. And I think even if I'd only done a small segment of what I'd planned, I think it would have been worthwhile because it made me look at what the needs might be within my students that I could have a personal impact on within the school year. It made me take a look at myself and at my teaching and what I could work on. (Adams, 2004, p. 113)

In passing it might be helpful to observe how this teacher was not using an officially prescribed technique based on research studies (knowledge above the teacher), but was calling on the knowledge gained from experience, the knowledge inside her, to construct new approaches to her teaching. The tone of her reflections represents a deep commitment to her students, and to a dialogical working relationship with them, thus indicating professional growth on both the first and the third leg of the model outlined above. In honoring these interests, the teacher practices the good of the teaching profession. While the results are seldom perfect, a community of teachers' continuous practice of attending to these interests cumulatively over twelve or thirteen years produces the "good" of a reasonably well educated person who is ready to take charge of her or his life, participate responsibly in public life, take on full membership in the worlds of nature, society, and culture.

The model can easily be incorporated in the work of cultivating an ethical school. It suggests that teachers need to continuously improve their dialogical knowledge on all three legs of the triangle. For some teachers that might mean a year or two additional learning about special needs children and how better to respond to them. For other teachers that might mean a year or two devoted to a greater personal understanding of the science embedded in the curriculum he or she teaches. For still others, it may mean a year working in a new team to develop appropriate rubrics for assessing student work. For teachers feeling the intense pressure to map their teaching to the state curriculum standards, that may mean developing a personal understanding of the knowledge required by the standards in order to reconstruct his or her teaching in such a way that students can encounter that material in a dialogical learning process and engage in the five kinds of learning within that dialogue.

Virtues that Facilitate the Ethical Work of Teaching

Virtues are ways of engaging the good that one is seeking. They are ways of achieving those internal goods which extend our human reach toward becoming more fully human. An earlier inquiry into the virtues that seem intrinsically tied to the work of educating and leading a process of educating proposed three virtues that seemed especially important in realizing the goods of learning and teaching: the virtue of presence, the virtue of authenticity, and the virtue of responsibility (Starratt, 2004). The final part of this chapter explores—all too briefly—how those virtues hold up when placed against the moral landscape of learning and teaching we have been considering.

The Virtue of Presence

One has to be present to the material or topic under study. Presence implies a dialogical relationship between the learner and the material under study. As with two persons, their mutual presence to each other makes a relationship possible, a relationship bonded by telling and listening. Each person listens to the other's words, taking them in, and with the words, taking the other person inside as one interprets what the other's words mean. The listener then responds to the other, presenting in the response both the listener's interpretation of what the other has said, and also how the listener responds from his or her perspective or feelings to what the other has said. Thus the dialogue goes back and forth with each person disclosing more of themselves and taking in richer and fuller understandings of the other. If one of the parties to the dialogue becomes distracted and fails to be fully attentive to the other person then the mutuality of presence is diminished, if not broken, and the integrity of the dialogue and the relationship that was developing is put in jeopardy

The practice of the virtue of presence in the process of learning is something that itself is learned. Some teachers will explicitly teach it under the guise of study skills, or creating a readiness set at the beginning of class. There are ways of getting the learners' attention, motivating them to focus and concentrate in anticipation of learning something of personal value to them. As the lesson progresses, teachers increase the learner's attention by posing new questions, "If x is thus and so, what does that imply for y?" or "What does this situation suggest for its resolution?" "Put yourself in this character's place. How would you reply? What would you do?" The point behind the questions is to encourage the learner to listen to the intelligibility embedded in the subject matter talking back to the learner, and inviting the learner to respond with her own understanding of the issue. The teacher is suggesting ways for the learner to be present to that intelligibility and to be open to taking that inside her own personal world.

While there are many nuances to being present, three seem particularly apropos in the activity of learning: (1) affirming presence, (2) enabling presence, and (3) critical presence. Affirming presence accepts the person or the event as it is, in its ambiguity, its incompleteness, it particularity, its multidimensionality. Enabling presence is open to the possibilities of the person or event to contain or reveal something special, something of deep value and significance. Critical presence expects to find both negative and positive features in persons and events. People and events and circumstances reveal unequal relationships of power and reciprocity. Critical presence brings to light what is tacit, assumed, or presumed in situations that reflect human constructions and beliefs. All of these ways of being present to what is being studied energize the dialogue between learners and one or more of the worlds under consideration in that unit of the curriculum. Those kinds of presence of the learner to those worlds enable those worlds to illuminate how the learner is already a member of those worlds, affirming something of the learner's identity, enabling the learner to become more fully him/her self, and as critiquing inappropriate assumptions and presumptions about their mutual relationships.

A second virtue that honors the integrity of learning is authenticity. The virtue of authenticity involves human beings in their most basic moral challenge, namely the challenge to be true to themselves, to be real. The opposite of that virtue is inauthenticity, playing false, making believe one is someone other than who one is. As with presence, the virtue of authenticity is a dialogical virtue. One cannot be authentic alone locked up in a closet. One is authentic in relationship to another. Authenticity is revealed in our words and actions, in our acting out the various social and cultural roles we play. Most basically one is authentic as a human being in response to the humanity of the other. One is also authentic as a son or daughter, as a friend or lover, a father and a mother. In all of these roles, one strives to be real, not a fake or cardboard character. But the expression of our authenticity has to take into account the similar effort of others to be true to themselves as well. Authenticity supposes a kind of social contract, namely, that if I expect a certain latitude to be myself, to own my life and my choices, so too must I afford to others the latitude to chart the courses of their own lives (Taylor, 1992).

The practice of ethical teaching asks the learner that he or she acknowledge the world as it is and to recognize that the learner's integrity is connected to the learner's relationship to the physical, social, and cultural worlds he or she is studying. Those worlds invite the learner into membership. Membership, however, imposes a recognition both of the benefits, and privileges, as well as responsibilities of membership. In other words, one's authenticity as a member of these worlds requires an understanding of the ways these worlds work. Understanding, however, does not always equal approval. Corruption in the world of politics is a familiar possibility. Recognizing that, one confronts the reality about politics as potentially corrupt, and therefore in need of critical participation. Racism is a reality in the social world. One's membership in the social world requires a critical stance toward that reality. Arrogant elitism based on class, wealth, or social standing is a feature of the cultural world. One's membership in a cultural world has to deal with the distorted stereotypes bred by that elitism. The learner pursues a way of being real, a way of expressing her or his goodness always in relationship to the realities of the worlds he or she inhabit.

The practice of the virtues of presence and authenticity in one's pedagogy imply a third virtue that seeks the goods of the learning process – the virtue of responsibility. It is a virtue exercised by teachers by being responsible to what one is teaching about in the worlds of nature, society, culture, and history. This virtue is enacted in two ways. First, in the teaching process itself, the teacher adopts an attitude of responsibility toward the material under study, whether it be the genetic code, the physics of magnets, a poem of Wordsworth, an historical account of the crusades, a novel by William Faulkner, the geography of Egypt or the geometry of architecture. These curricular elements reveal how humans have interpreted and represented aspects of the natural, the social, the cultural, and the historical worlds. The teacher has a responsibility to work with the learners to get inside the realities being represented in those curriculum units, to grasp the value or the intelligibility, or the perspective (or conflict of perspectives), or the multiple implications and applications to be drawn from those curriculum units. In other words, the teacher takes seriously her or his responsibility to bring students ever closer to the truth (and its opposites), the beauty (and its opposites), the values (and their opposites), the reasonableness (and its contradictions) illuminated by those curriculum units as well as the connections to aspects of the students' lives. The second way the virtue of responsibility is exercised by teachers is more of a proactive responsibility to the learners in one's charge to refuse to give up on their potential to learn. That sense of responsibility continually asks of the teacher to uncover the reason for students' underperformance. That sense of responsibility is a challenge to the teacher's sense of efficacy, namely, that there is no learning difficulty that she cannot find the answer to. If students are not learning, then the teacher may have to go back to the drawing board *with the student* to find out where the blockage or the misunderstandings began, or what motivations, or life connections can be uncovered, and more appropriate learning activities designed.

Teachers, moreover, should begin to link the moral character of their work to the moral character of learning. That is, they need to teach these very virtues of presence and authenticity and responsibility as virtues that cultivate the good of learning, both by explicitly developing the learners' study skills, attitudes and methods of inquiry, and implicitly in the way they, the teachers, model their approach to the study of these worlds. They should be modeling their sense of presence to the complexity, beauty, and challenges of the biophysical, cultural, and social worlds; their sense of authenticity in dialogue with the truths of these worlds; and their sense of responsibility to and for these worlds. This aspect of teachers' ethical work deserves a treatment of its own. For the moment, suffice it to say that the work will require so much more than preparing young people to paint by numbers in getting them to construct the right answers to someone else's questions on high stakes tests.

Summary

This chapter has attempted to expound a view of teaching as a special kind of moral activity, an activity, therefore, that needs its own special ethical analysis and its own chapter among scholarly summaries of special or professional ethics. In claiming a special view of its moral goods and the virtues that promote those goods, educational leaders can appeal to the wider public that supports the practice of teaching and benefits from it to honor the moral integrity that learning and teaching entail and request that misguided policies that distort or frustrate that integrity be amended. Furthermore, we have to remember that the special moral integrity of education, as with all other professions, will always be situated within those larger frameworks by which morality in all its special forms receives its ultimate legitimation, namely, the frameworks of the general ethics of justice, care, and critique. Those ethics not only legitimate the special concerns of different professions and practices, they are the tap roots, so to speak, which give them an enduring vitality.

Currently, the policy emphasis on curriculum standards is being driven by the assumption (along with an exclusively cognitive brand of psychology) that schools should be teaching learners to think like mathematicians, scientists, historians, literary critics (Wiske, 1998). This exclusive focus is misguided on two counts. First, as evidenced by high stakes testing protocols, it concentrates the work of the schools almost entirely, mission statements to the contrary notwithstanding, on the cognitive development of learners, to the neglect of the psycho-social development of learners, thereby sacrificing some of the most important goods of the learning process. Second, in its efforts to turn learners into mini scholars, it turns schools into university prep schools. A tiny fraction of the learners in a given nation's schools will become academic scholars. The upper years of college and graduate school will take care of preparing the scholar academicians, and the highly specialized professionals. *All* learners in our public schools, however, will become adult citizens. The focus on the goods of learning ought to be concerned primarily with learning—within and across the academic subject areas—what young people need to know as human beings, as citizens who vote, who debate public policy, who have to manage households and participate in neighborhood projects, who have to learn to live with and learn from people and groups who are different in many ways from them, and contribute to the common weal in their careers and leisure activities. As a foundation for that kind of citizenship, schools need to promote through the academic subject areas, co-curriculars, and student support services, what young people need to learn to become intelligent, responsible, self-fulfilled, healthy, other-connected, compassionate, and mature human beings who can participate, contribute, and find fulfillment in various dimensions of democratic public life. That should be the ultimate moral good pursued by the profession of education in the nation's public schools.

CHAPTER 8

Elements of an Ethical School

The previous chapters have attempted to develop various crucial elements that would make up an ethical school, or a system of ethical schools. This chapter will attempt to position those elements in a somewhat logical order, along with additional commentary that will in summary fashion highlight their importance. The effort here is to bring the main points of the preceding chapters, each of which involved some conceptual heavy lifting, into a certain clarity and applicability. It will become evident that we are presenting an idealized picture of what a school or a system of schools belonging to a single school district or school authority might look like in its full development. Such a picture is intended to lay out for those educators who might want to actually attempt to cultivate an ethical school or school system what elements would more thoroughly guarantee its integrity.

Let me say at the outset that cultivating an ethical school such as I am suggesting would not necessarily involve a wholesale change in the way schools are normally conducted. My assumption is that many, if not most schools would have some of the elements already in place, at least implicitly. On the other hand, cultivating an ethical school would involve changing assumptions embedded in many of the current practices, changes that would qualitatively transform those practices into something richer and more complex. My wager is that in many cases, schools could get a "two-fer"—that is, could continue to satisfy an existing goal while adding value to an existing practice. It will become clearer as the chapter unfolds how deep and extensive a change may be involved as readers imagine these elements being included into the culture and structures of their own schools.

Cultivating an ethical school will require important elements to be present in the life of the school such as those that follow.

1 A clear mission statement that will provide a compass for the activities, operations, and policies of the school.
2 A foundation in both general and professional ethical perspectives.
3 A foundation in a theory of human development.
4 A foundation in a learning theory that will guide the pedagogy of the school.
5 An academic, social and civic curriculum that is consistent with the school's theory of learning.
6 Teachers and administrators who are committed to the work of such a school.
7 Working relationships with the home and the local community.
8 Ethical organizational policies, structures, and procedures.
9 An ethical school culture.
10 Ethical outcomes.

Rationale for a Clear School Mission Statement

Traditionally, schools, and the practice of teaching which is supposed to go on within their walls have claimed a certain mission, and therefore a certain legitimacy in the public arena. That mission involves the three-fold concentration on the intellectual development, the civic development, and the personal development of the students in their charge. With that in mind, let us attempt to unpack the ingredients of this threefold mission as it applies to teachers' work.

One may consider the practice of teaching as having three differing legitimizing perspectives:

1) Teachers teach the study of an academic discipline in order to develop new members of the community that practice that discipline (e.g., biology, computer graphics, geography, geology, constitutional law).

1a) Through involvement with the academic curriculum, the novice researcher/performer adopts an identity of a scholar/performer (e.g., as a microbial biologist, an historian, a social psychologist, a sculptor). That is, the learner has been exposed and involved during his or her school years with that academic discipline to the point where the learner aspires to pursue a certain mastery of that discipline as the basis for a career. Many students in their K-12 school years, however, will be satisfied with a general process of intellectual development across many academic disciplines that provide him or her with a foundation for later choices in further education or in various jobs in specific career choices. The school will have fulfilled its mission in either case by activating the development of intellectual inquiry about how the world works and about a variety of possible life trajectories for the learners in their charge.

2) Teachers teach the study of an academic discipline in order to develop knowledgeable citizens who can apply the knowledge and understanding of the discipline to current cultural and political issues and public policy debate. E.g., applying knowledge from biological studies to issues around personal and public health and environmental sustainability; applying knowledge of classical Greek drama to a critical appraisal of a contemporary production of a Greek classic; applying a critical knowledge of child labor practices during the Industrial Revolution in Europe to present practices involving child labor in developing nations; understanding of constitutional law and its application to present debatable issues (e.g., the rights of immigrants; rights of gay partners in a marriage).

2a) The practice of citizenship realizes the good of sociality, of mutuality, of distributive justice, of civic participation and generativity, of appreciation of expressions of cultural diversity, of the pursuit of the common good and the protection of civil and human rights.

2b) The practice of that discipline is carried out by citizens as neighbors, as members of a local civic community, as members of political parties, as members of voluntary service organizations, as workers in various corporate and governmental organizations, as participants in cultural events and members of cultural organizations.

2c) The virtues associated with the practice of citizenship are responsibility to protect public resources and promote the common good; respect for diverse opinions and cultural expressions; protection and promotion of human and civil rights; participation in upholding and promoting community cultural values; participation in public policy debates and election of public officials.

2d) Through involvement with the academic curriculum (as well as student life in the school), the novice citizen internalizes the role and activities of a citizen as part of one's identity.

3) Teachers teach the study of the academic disciplines in order to nurture the growth of students toward a fuller humanity and personhood as a member of and participant in the cultural, the social and the bio-physical worlds. Membership and participation in the worlds of culture, society and nature is where one's personal identity is discovered, engaged, constructed, challenged, rebuffed, or/and fulfilled. The academic disciplines provide windows toward those worlds: the world of culture through the study of language, art, music, cuisine, dress, traditions, values, architecture, technology, rituals, philosophical and religious perspectives; the

world of society through the study of history, anthropology, sociology, political science, law, economics, psychology and social psychology; the world of nature through the sciences of physics, chemistry and biology, and the applied sciences of medicine, agronomy, botany, oceanography, engineering, geography, astronomy, and so forth. The overarching goal of the teacher is to stimulate the student to ask of the academic material being studied: "How do these studies help me to know myself, who I am, how my physical, cultural and social make-up works, how I fit into this world, what this world asks of me, how is this world already in me and I already in this world, what does this material suggest I'm supposed to do with my life, how do I participate in this world with this knowledge"—all questions flowing from the often asked question, "Why do we have to study this, anyway?" "What's it got to do with MY life?"

3a) The discipline of learning at this level involves introspection, discussion, interpretation, imagination, self-criticism, criticism of the worlds one inhabits, exploration of roles, careers, values, life trajectories. The methodology includes journaling, creative expression, role taking, and role invention, trial and error, conversation with multiple others, philosophical rumination, moral questioning.

3b) The good cultivated and realized by this learning is the fuller development of the increasingly mature human being as a human person.

3c) The virtues associated with this kind of learning are the practice of authenticity, presence, responsibility, patience, courage, creativity.

3d) Through involvement with the academic curriculum the young learner continues the journey of self-understanding and personal identity construction which leads to a mature adulthood of a complete human being.

This threefold mission of the school and of the work of teaching often is expressed in three distinct organizational divisions of the school, namely the academic curriculum, the curriculum of student life and co-curricular activities, and the curriculum of the counseling and psychological services. Indeed, those three units of the school as an organization take it upon themselves to serve the threefold mission of the school. However, they tend to function as separate silos, with little or no intentional connection among them. Yet, the academic curriculum should speak to the intelligibility of various aspects of citizenship, and to the intelligibility of self-discovery, self-commitment, self-expression, and membership in the worlds of culture, society, and nature. Otherwise, the academic curriculum can be incorrectly seen as a world unto itself, having little or no relationship to one's public, civic life, or to one's personal journey into self-understanding. The promotion of the connection among the three foci of the mission of the school does not mean subjecting the integrity of the academic disciplines to political ideologies, or to personal counseling and navel gazing. Instead, it implies that the academic curriculum should continually explore the intelligibility of the worlds of culture, society, and nature as the arenas where human life is lived, where humans make their way and make their mark. Involvement with the intelligibility of academic subjects is not an end in itself, but rather a means of understanding the human context and the human predicament, enacting that understanding to collectively make our way in our historical moment, with its challenges and promise.

There is much talk about preparing young people to work and to live in the knowledge economy, as though the knowledge economy is some impersonal cosmic force that has fallen from the sky and humans have little choice but to subject themselves to its discipline and pace and exponential information overload. The knowledge economy, however, is a human invention, and it is up to humans to decide how to live a human community and personal life within a knowledge economy. Thus, it becomes increasingly important to honor the integrity of the civic curriculum, and the personal curriculum in schools in much closer relationship to the academic curriculum, lest schools fail in their mission to nurture in the next generation those skills and understanding concerning their civic and human responsibilities in relation to a knowledge economy.

If the school has no available mission statement, one should be presented to the faculty for a vote. That mission statement should clearly express the three-fold focus of the school's mission. All members of the school community should examine their practice in the light of the school mission as part of their annual performance assessment. Administrators in the school should see that the mission statement or references to it should be included in important messages to the school community, including the students and parents.

Foundation in General and Professional Ethics

Administrators, teachers, counselors and all other support staff should be committed to treating one another and the youngsters in their care from the perspectives of the ethics of care, justice, and critique. They should all have had an opportunity to review their understandings and applications of these ethics in seminars and in readings every two or three years, and consider that their ethical commitments are part of their contract with the school. From time to time, as cases emerge, they should have the opportunity to discuss their responses to the cases from the perspective of those three ethics. Administrators, especially, should review school policies and operations from the perspective of the ethic of critique in order to ensure that some school policies or operations do not advantage some members of the school community, while disadvantaging others.

All new members of the school staff should become familiar with the professional ethics of the educating community—their obligation to prevent harm while engaging in their professional practice, and their obligation to promote the good of the learning process for the younger members of the community, in so far as that good is spelled out in the mission of the school. Periodically, faculty will be invited to share examples of how the good of learning is manifested in the work of their students. Innovative efforts in curriculum design that exemplify how various curriculum units are promoting students' connecting that material to their lives outside of school should be shared among the faculty. New members of the faculty should attend workshops illustrating those curriculum unit designs taught by veteran members of the faculty during the pre-tenure years of the newcomers. Faculty mentors working with new teachers during their pre-tenure years should assist the new teachers in trying out various curriculum unit designs that will promote one or more of the three learnings referred to in the school's mission statement.

A Foundation in a Theory of Human Development

At the beginning of each school year, teachers will be encouraged to review the anxieties students face with a new teacher and challenging work ahead of them. They will need to gain a trusting relationship with the teacher, need encouragement to exercise a certain autonomy in their learning process, encouragement to explore where the new learning demands might lead them, what new skills they will need to develop to master the tasks they'll be working on, how the various curriculum units will open up new aspects of their membership in the worlds of nature, culture, and society. The teachers will need to model the virtues of authenticity, presence and responsibility as they encourage the youngsters to work together with them on the year's adventures and journeys.

Whether in an elementary, middle, or secondary school, teachers will be sensitive to their students' need for attention and respect in their working relationship with their teachers, their need for differentiated and culturally responsive instruction, for constructive feedback, for opportunities to explore their relationship to the natural, cultural and social worlds they belong to, and to the ways they can perform their membership in those worlds.

Again, mentors for the new teachers will provide guidance in developing these kinds of sensitivities and responses to their students, encouraging them to open up the possible connections between the curriculum and the students' lives.

A Foundation in a Learning Theory That Will Guide the Pedagogy of the School

At the beginning of every school year, teachers will review the learning theory that will guide their pedagogy. That learning theory is the key to the success of the ethical school, for it connects the moral agenda of the learner to become a somebody to the moral character of their learning to become members of the cultural, natural, and social worlds while engaging with the academic, social, and civic curriculum of the school. That learning theory positions the learner as the key worker, with the teacher as a guide, a motivator, and a coach. The teacher works to design learning activities that stimulate a dialogue between the learner and the realities under study. That dialogue tacitly brings the intelligibility of the curriculum unit into the world of the learner, illuminating the learner's relationship to the world and raising a sense of membership in the world, a membership that supports or challenges his or her identity and incurs rights in and responsibilities to that world.

Teachers will be encouraged to review those curriculum units that worked well in the past and those that need improvement in the coming year. Teachers will be encouraged to share their successes and their shortcomings in their curriculum designs so they might borrow ideas from one another. They will be reminded that part of their annual evaluation will be concerned with the new unit designs they have developed that better encourage the desired dialogue between the student and curriculum, as well as exemplars of student assessments on those units.

Administrators and teachers will also discuss needed improvements in the social and civic curriculum that will complement their gains in the academic curriculum. These discussions will explore connections between the learnings across all three curricula, seeking to reinforce those connections to important life lessons.

An Academic, Social, and Civic Curriculum That Is Consistent With the School's Theory of Learning

At the elementary, middle and secondary levels, each school will have articulated the large learning goals that will comprise the outcomes of each grade of the school. While those outcomes will be listed separately as academic learning outcomes, social learning outcomes, and civic learning outcomes, there will be explicit connections both horizontally across the academic, social, and civic curricula, and vertical connections with the outcomes of grades preceding and following the outcomes of each grade. At the beginning, middle and end of each school year, these outcomes will be reviewed, and each teacher will be expected to provide examples of how they will attend to or have attended to these outcomes, and how students are making or not making progress on these goals. These discussions will also facilitate discussions between teachers and parents at the beginning, middle, and end of the school year, as well as provide perspectives or frameworks for school assessments of student learnings during the school year.

Obviously, the above attention to these grade level outcomes can become a nightmare when they become ends rather than means of promoting quality learning for each child. It should be expected that each child will reflect a different profile of success or growth toward these school outcomes, a profile influenced not only by the teacher's expertise and hard work, but also by multiple home variables, health variables, opportunities to learn variables, and so forth. Furthermore, the fine tuning of assessments and their analysis can become progressively distracting from the ongoing work of instruction and the engagement of students in the sequence of the learning activities. Remediation is often simplistically thought of as having to go back and repeat all the steps in the prior learning activities, instead of involving a finer concentration in the next sequence of learning activities on avoiding the mistakes made during the prior curriculum unit. In other words, learning defects can be corrected as the weeks and months unfold with new curriculum units, rather than insisting on after-school remediation of the problematic material. Providing teachers time to work in groups to discuss student work can provide the generation of ideas for attending to prior misunderstandings or mistakes on previous assessments in the new material at hand. Attention to micro perfection can get in the way of progress on the larger learning goals.

In the school's attempts to relate learnings in the academic, social, and civic curricula to one another, teachers and administrators might choose two or three connected learning outcomes per semester for each grade level. Each outcome might involve, for example, a unit in the science curriculum that could be connected with a student application in one or more student life projects, and with an application to an aspect of the student government. For example, a unit in biology that studied the effect of sugar in the diet on diabetes and obesity might be connected to a survey of students in that grade level's consumption of sugar in the number of soft drinks they consume in a normal week. In turn, the students might bring the results of their survey to the attention of the student government with the recommendation for discussions with the school's administration concerning their sponsorship of a larger study of the student body's consumption of sugared soft drinks during a normal week. The results of that study might lead to the school's limiting the kind of soft drinks available in the school's cafeteria, and sending a message to the parents urging them to limit the availability of sugared soft drinks at home. These activities could easily lead to further exploration of the kinds of preservatives embedded in the food they eat in the school cafeteria, and their long term effects on their bodies.

Another example might be based on a social studies unit on prejudice in the United States during the Nineteenth and Twentieth Centuries. This unit covered a variety of exhibitions of prejudice: racial, ethnic, sexual, religious, and class. The class had reviewed historical examples, the prejudice against people of African descent, Asians, Native Americans, and all indigenous peoples; against Jews, Catholics, Muslims, Hindus; against women, gays, and lesbians; against Irish, Italians, Mexicans, Hispanics; against the working class, servants, and indigent people, against people with mental and physical handicaps. These prejudices are expressed in demeaning stereotypes and labels. They influence voting rights, job and career opportunities, educational opportunities, housing patterns, access to health care, religious freedom, membership in organizations and private associations. Their worst expressions involve violence, humiliation, oppressive divisions of power, and genocide. Having been exposed to many examples of the above, students are encouraged to (1) examine their own practices and expressions of prejudice; (2) examine prejudicial expressions and opinions harbored by their families; and (3) to list the various off-hand prejudicial or stereotypical labels they hear in school, arranging them in the order of frequency and virulence. They then get together and discuss the severity of each of these prejudices and explore how to respond to these examples of real prejudice. They take the results of their discussions to the administration and to the student government for some kind of school-wide response. Furthermore, each student would be required to compose a reflection on their personal learnings in this unit for their language arts class as well as their social studies class.

Both of these examples of connecting learnings in the academic, the social, and the civic curriculum of the school point to ways in which the academic learnings can expose learners to their membership in the world of nature, society and culture, and to the responsibilities membership implies. Not every effort needs to be connected to *both* the social and the civic curriculum; connection to one or the other will suffice in some cases. I believe that the learnings will have a greater impact, however, when they are connected to all three.

Furthermore, the learnings in the social and civic curriculum of the school do not have to be confined within the walls of the school. The school should have the annual calendar of activities of various organizations in the community—the various not-for-profit organizations that focus on a variety of community issues such as the Sierra Club, the League of Women Voters, civil rights organizations, The Chamber of Commerce, the Elks Club, environmental sustainability organizations, The Urban League, the local YMCA/YWCA and Boys and Girls Clubs, artistic venues, sponsored lectures at local bookstores, junior colleges, libraries, trade associations, and so forth. Teachers can identify a lecture series, or a meeting of citizens that pertain to the core idea or issue of a curriculum unit. The school can also invite speakers from the community to address their class on a topic associated with the curriculum unit they are dealing with. In some instances the academic lesson can be connected to various school outreach activities, such as a musical performance at a nursing home, the design and composition of birthday cards to be sent to elderly shut-ins, carrying on email connections with students their age in overseas countries. As well, a wealth of resources are available over the internet to bring out a civic application of the lessons in the curriculum.

Besides the academic examples cited, one can easily conjure up other possibilities stimulated by learnings in literature and the arts, mathematics and history, and any of the sciences. This kind of involvement in the design of academic units connected to the social and civic curriculum life-lessons enables the teachers themselves to participate in their own rights and responsibilities as members in the worlds of nature, culture, and society. These activities tend to illuminate the significance of the ethics of care, justice, and critique *in practice.*

These illustrations do not have to be multiplied tenfold, in ways that would inappropriately crowd out other units of the curriculum. On the other hand, if every academic subject on its own, or combined with one or two other academic subjects, had to involve at least one of its curriculum units per year in connection with the social and civic curriculum of the school, then students would begin to be exposed to two, perhaps three of these large learning activities that tie the academic to the social and civic lives of the students every year. Over a ten to twelve year exposure to these kinds of learnings embedded in "real" life, it would be bound to leave a lasting impression of how the schooling process introduces them to the rights and responsibilities of their membership in the world.

One can begin to gain a feel for the power of learnings connecting the academic curriculum to the social world of the student and the civic world of inside the school self-governance as well as the civic world in the larger community. The abstractions of the academic curriculum are illuminated by and connected to the pulsing life and challenges of the young learners, and to the adult world of the civic community. The moral agenda of the young person to see herself as an actor on the stage of real life, as belonging to something important, something that needs her talents and abilities, something stimulating her to imagine an adult identity, well beyond the sterile agenda of grade-getting, is connected to the moral character of the learning activities themselves, activities that engage not only her mind, but her whole person. This is learning that has some integrity to it, learning that is connected to the ethics of membership in the world.

Teachers and Administrators Who Are Committed to the Work of Such a School

Obviously, a school such as we have been talking about, as well as a school system that embodies the same ideals, will be impossible without teachers and administrators who are committed to this type of ethical educational process. The cultivation of such a school starts there. In some cases there will already exist a significant number of teachers and administrators who, though lacking the precise vocabulary employed in this book, will have a tacit or intuitive understanding of and commitment to this educational ideal. In that case, this book can help to provide the vocabulary and the rationale for pushing that agenda forward. In other cases, there may be a minority of teachers and administrators who struggle to create some movement in this direction but who find themselves boxed in by the narrow concentration on raising scores on state exams. Depending very much on the leadership of the school system, they may begin to find a way in adding value to that major focus on test scores through individual efforts and the slow progress of winning over more and more teachers and school authorities to these value-added initiatives. There may be an individual principal in a school district that will want to initiate this effort in her or his school who may gain permission to start this effort as a pilot project. That will require encouraging teachers in the school to buy into adopting the beginning elements described in this chapter and working over five years to show the rest of the schools in the district the advantages of cultivating this kind of school.

Working Relationships With the Home and the Local Community

Each school should have a variety of home–school communications, both electronic and print. Parents of students coming to the school for the first time should be briefed early in the year about the learning theory and human development theory behind the efforts of the school to become an ethical school. Parents of all the students will receive periodic encouragements to discuss their children's response to the major learning activities that connect the academic, social, and civic curricula as they are interspersed throughout the semester. Parents will also be encouraged to appropriately echo other examples of engaging the social and civic curricula in conversations with their children. Children are more likely to absorb those lessons when they see their parents taking an interest. Parents are more likely to be supportive when they see the school inviting them to participate as partners in their children's learning. Citizen volunteer associations in the community are more likely to support the school's efforts when they are invited to partner with the school in the civic curriculum.

Ethical Organizational Policies, Structures, and Procedures

Administrators and teachers will hold discussions at least once a semester concerning how their operating procedures, structures, and policies exemplify caring, just and critical ethical perspectives. It would be hypocritical of a school to expect children to learn ethical lessons when the school itself does not function ethically. For example, schools need a fair teacher appraisal system, one that refuses to blame teachers as the sole cause of student underperformance. Schools need to ask themselves whether the one-size-fits-all class time, daily and weekly schedule, textbooks, assessment systems, assignment of letter grades with no formative feedback on what the grades signify—whether the way the school functions provides students an adequate opportunity to learn the material that gets tested, or even an opportunity to finish the tests in the time allotted; whether the teachers have sufficient opportunity to teach the material being tested; whether the material being taught has any significance to the students, whether the home situation is so chaotic as to inhibit learning. In other words, the school organization or home variables may be at least as much an influence on student underperformance as the quality of the instruction. Likewise, the school needs to look at the fairness of averaging scores on homework, quizzes and tests throughout a grading period, rather than assigning a grade that reflects the quality of the student's work toward the end of the grading period when the student would have had a chance to improve his performance, having learned from his early efforts where he or she was making mistakes. Also, the practice of teachers grading on a "normal curve" tends to reflect the way the test or assignment was designed, rather than a fair opportunity for all students to show what they had learned. These are but a few examples of how the school unfairly treats its students and teachers. It will be an uphill struggle for a school to make much headway in improving the moral character of teaching and learning when it provides contrary examples of unfairness to its members in its own organizational structures and procedures.

An Ethical School Culture

A school's internal culture—"the way things are done around here"—can be open or closed, individualistic or communal, competitive or collaborative, bureaucratic or democratic, monocultural or multicultural. A school culture that might be characterized as closed, monocultural, bureaucratic, individualistic, and competitive would present problems to initiatives seeking to engage the moral character of learning and teaching as we describe learning and teaching in this book. Again, that kind of culture would contradict the kinds of lessons the school was trying to teach. This obviously suggests that school leaders would have to examine their school culture before trying to cultivate an ethical school.

Ethical Outcomes

Finally, one could quickly identify a school as ethical by the way people in the school treated one another, by the messages posted on the bulletin board, by its communications with parents, by its overall curriculum, by its award system, by the way its students and its graduates carried themselves in the wider community, by the school's general reputation in the community.

Measuring One's School or School District/System Against the Elements of an Ethical School

At this point we might pause and reflect on how our own school or school district measures up against the above elements of an ethical school. On the assumption that most readers working in a school system might already find themselves in a school or school system that reflected some of the approaches recommended in this book, let me suggest that you rate your school or school system on a 0 to 10 scale (10 being the highest) against each of the ten elements. The rating would not require that you used the same vocabulary as found in this book. Rather, think more of the substance of what the book is conveying about each element and rate what you think is, in one form or another, presently being enacted in a fairly frequent or infrequent way in your school or school system. Try to give two or three examples of the kinds of things that might lead you to give that score. I doubt there would be any school that would rate itself a score of 100. I would consider a score of 30 or 40 quite promising. That would seem to indicate a foundation to build on. A score of 50 or 60 would show a school well along the way. When you have rated your school or school system on each of the elements, step back and look at the strengths you have identified, and then the shortcomings. What kind of pattern emerges? Is there a clear mission statement to build on? Are the efforts concentrated in one or two academic areas, or grade clusters? Are some teachers really strong and many not so strong on connecting their academics to ethical issues? Is the culture of the school supportive of including explicit ethical lessons throughout the school's activities?

Ask yourself whether answers to these questions point toward some short term and long term initiatives that can increase the focus on ethical learning in the life of the school. Perhaps these ruminations are worth sharing with people at your school. Discuss your findings with your classmates. How do your findings compare with theirs? If you were in charge of your school, how would the ideas in this book influence the substance and the style of your leadership?

CHAPTER 9

Cultivating an Ethical School

(CO-AUTHORED WITH M. BEZZINA)

As the prior chapter suggests, cultivating an ethical school is an organic endeavor. That is, the ethical character of the educational process is not an add-on to an already tossed salad of organizational ingredients. Rather, the ethical character of the educational process has to do with the integrity of the whole enterprise. As such, it should permeate the purpose and process of every element in the school: the academic program, the student life program, the counseling program, the policy guidelines and procedures, the school culture, the school pedagogy and assessments, the organizational structure, the home-school program, the co-curricular program, the interscholastic programs. That means that in all elements and aspects of the school's life, specific lessons about autonomy, connectedness, and transcendence should be taught. Likewise, all elements and aspects of the school life should be managed with and should reflect an ethic of care, justice, and critique.

This chapter is addressed to those professionals with primary responsibility to attend to the ethical character of the school. In an ideal situation, that would include the district or system administrators, the individual school administrators, teachers, counselors and other professional staff. We should be careful not to exclude the primary workers in the school, the students and their student leaders. The school will reflect its ethical character if the students' activities—in the classroom, the cafeteria, the playing fields, and in their neighborhoods—are imbued with autonomy, connectedness, and transcendence, and guided by the ethic of care, justice, and critique. As a school turns its attention to the various elements of an ethical school, students should be encouraged to participate in the process in ways appropriate to their own human development and standing in the school.

All educators should be wary of outside experts arriving at their school with plans and blueprints for improving or transforming their school. The research on such approaches to school change indicates that changes imposed from the top or from outside stand a meager chance of effecting what they advertise. This book has no intention of providing a plan that any or many schools should adopt. On the other hand, the book was not intended to fill out a reading list for a graduate school course, only to be tossed aside when the final grades are posted. Rather, I see it as providing ideas for vision of the schooling process for a wide audience—professors, teachers, school administrators, curriculum directors, school board members, policy workers—that might align with and reinforce some of their own ideas. Those initial connections might lead to conversations with like-minded educators to explore how those ideas might be applied in their own work, and in a school or school system, or a school of education they belonged to. Through an unpredictable network of conversations, I would hope that this book would play a part, however small, in a variety of intentional "cultivations" of ethical schools.

But first let me spell out some smaller scale imaginary scenarios that some readers might identify with. We will conclude with a description of a large scale effort that is actually under way.

Three Imaginary Scenarios

In the first imaginary scenario, let's say that you are a full-time secondary teacher who is taking a course in a graduate program at a nearby university, and this book is a textbook for the course. Let us suppose that you resonate with the ideas about connecting your teaching of history to the issues communities like those your students come from are confronting. You might explore how a unit that you will be teaching in the coming month actually could be redesigned as a trial of these ideas. Perhaps you belong to a social studies department that is quite traditional and would not be interested in following your example. Nevertheless, you believe you owe it to your own students to stir up some interest in recognizing that history is about folks like them caught up in these kinds of challenges. Let us suppose that you go ahead on your own and construct several learning activities that will help your students connect the unit with their lives and the lives of those in their community. Further, suppose the students really caught on to the connections, and began to have conversations with their parents and fellow students about how history was happening in their lives, and that it would either happen to them *without* their participation, or it would happen *with* their participation. Let us suppose that, further, your students began to ask for other history units that were connected to issues in their lives. Now you have a challenge. You can either retreat to the safe but boring ground of teaching history that happens to other people, or you can follow where this kind of authentic pedagogy takes you. In the latter choice, the book will have played a part in making a difference for the students in your class, in their sense of membership in the social world. Furthermore, you may never go back to your old way of teaching, whether you continue to teach at that school, or whether you go on to become a principal who promotes your new kind of teaching. That's one kind of life I'd like to see this book have.

In another scenario, let us suppose that you are a principal who is enrolled in a doctoral program at a nearby university. Let us suppose that you have taken a course in which this book was a required text. Let us suppose that the multiperspective framework of the ethic of care, justice, and critique has caught your attention, and while you give yourself high grades in the care and justice ethics, you are troubled by the ethic of critique. You never before realized your moral responsibility to protect students from the dysfunctional structures in the school that affect your students' *opportunity to learn* the material on the state tests, especially your second language and special needs learners. Furthermore, you see more clearly the injustice of your teachers being blamed for their students underperformance on state tests, when, in reality, the way the daily, weekly and semester schedules were arranged, many of your teachers never had sufficient *opportunities to teach* those underperforming students. In your school with its one-size-fits-all class schedules, textbooks, curriculum resources, and timed assessment system, groups of students and teachers were victimized by those arrangements, yet were blamed for the "poor" results. This realization has shaken your principal's ethical self-image. You realize that you have to address the structured injustice of this situation. Even before the course is completed, you have begun to have conversations with your teachers about revising the daily and weekly schedule so as to create more "opportunity to learn" classes for those who need it, and more "opportunities to teach" for teachers who need to provide more careful feedback and structure to their underperforming students. Furthermore, you recognize that for some of your brightest students, the school fails to provide enrichment learning opportunities. You therefore plan to have additional conversations with your staff about how the school schedule might accommodate enrichment opportunities for those students. You are fortunate enough to have the support of the superintendent who has encouraged you to create a school guided by the "opportunity to learn" mission that could be a pilot for the whole district to emulate.

That scenario would be another way for this book to live into the future.

Another scenario for the adventure of this book might involve a professor at a university school of education. You saw the book advertised, and since you had an interest in connecting social justice with the courses you teach in the curriculum and teaching department, you decided to purchase it and bring it along on your summer holiday reading. Let us say that you are captured by the book's focus on teaching the academic curriculum as the students' ongoing introduction to their membership in the worlds of nature, society, and culture. You explore ways you can introduce that idea into your course on elementary school curriculum development. You also see how you can frame that course as an introduction to your own prospective teachers of *their membership* in the community of educators. That would mean encouraging them to understand the basic ethic of teaching as connecting their relationship with the students and their relationship with the curriculum to the kinds of learning activity designs that enable the dialogue of students with the intelligibility embedded in the curriculum unit. Since the members of your department get together once a month to discuss a book or research report, you plan to suggest this book as a candidate for that activity. You see several possible applications of the ideas of the book for other courses being taught in your department. You also see its possible use for the program in educational leadership, and will share the book with one of your friends in that department. That scenario, introduced perhaps as wishful thinking, would also point to another journey with multiple audiences in the field of education.

A More Systematic Scenario

Besides the relatively haphazard adventures of the book imagined above, I would also propose another, more systematic use of the book. I could imagine a principal or a superintendent who, having read the book, appreciated the notion of cultivating an ethical school as a long term, somewhat systematic development of a school or a school system. I will begin with the scenario of the principal of a middle school.

Having read and reflected on the book, the principal decided to use the book as a part of her own self-assessment. Beginning with the first chapter, she decided she would go through each one and note the points she agreed with, and already had incorporated into her understanding of herself, as well as incorporated into some aspect of her practice. She would also note whether her school was reflecting in one or more ways the values and perspectives promoted in each chapter. This latter assessment would point, perhaps, to some initiatives she might consider.

Her reading of the first chapter gave her a headache. It was too much to absorb at one sitting, but she noted some ideas that struck her: Relationality as our essential reality, learning as relating to one's membership in the world, learning as dialogue with intelligibility, information speedway rather than highway, urgency of environmental studies, reflective rationality.

The reading of the second chapter began to give her a fix on the foundational qualities she could recognize as evident in the conversations she has with her students, but these conversations are with students in some kind of trouble, who are struggling to grow into those qualities. She began to see that the school needed to move beyond controlling prohibited behaviors to encouraging their more positive behavioral counterparts.

In reading the third chapter she realized that the school needed more explicit and continuous attention to the ethic of care. Along with this, she fixed on the notion of restorative justice as the more desired form of school responses to discipline problems. She wasn't sure what to make of the ethic of critique. Wasn't that the union's job?

The fourth chapter was helpful to recognize the importance of moving from the extrinsic reward and punishment shaping of behavior toward the positive reasons why the more mature behaviors were in tune with the person their youngsters wanted to become.

The connection of human development to moral development made sense. She could see how the industry stage characterized so much of the middle school agenda for the youngsters—learning the multiple skills, both social and academic, needed to perform as an adult.

The sixth chapter drew her into the meaning of learning as dialogue, learning as grasping one's relationality to and with the world, learning as recognizing membership and the responsibilities of participating as a member. Lots of work to be done here with teachers and curriculum development. Also assessment design and feedback. The ethics of teaching struck her as surprisingly simple: Care for each child; be passionate about the curriculum; bring knowledge of the child and knowledge of the curriculum into design of leaning activities that speak to the learners. Promote the GOOD of learning!!

The elements of an ethical school in chapter eight provided a good review, and a good set of criteria to assess the current health of the school. We seem to show some strengths, but have a ways to go.

Stepping back from the re-read of the book, the principal now saw how the professional ethics of promoting the good of learning helped to define the integrity of her work. She saw that she had a large agenda ahead of her. On the other hand, if spread out over three or four years, it was an agenda that could really change the whole quality of the student's experience at her school. That was what the good of learning was really all about.

She now began to prioritize in a brainstorming kind of way.

1 Begin with the school culture. Increase our efforts to promote a culture of community. The notion of membership, of belonging to a community where I can be a somebody. Membership brings belonging and also responsibility. All of this applies to teachers (all adults in the schools) as well as students and their parents and guardians. Begin some process of restorative justice for major discipline infractions. Tie it to membership ... belonging to a community. More involvement of parents, especially minority parents.

2 As cultural values become more explicit—lots more posters and community pictures around the school—revise the mission statement of the school to be more consistent with what we are trying to do.

3 Besides a culture of community, develop notion of a community of service, and a community of excellence—personal excellence as well as community excellence.

4 Start to develop themes of autonomy, connectedness, and transcendence through informal and then more formal discussions with the teachers and counselors.

5 Explore an auditing process that allows us to map where important lessons in the academic curriculum, the social curriculum of student life, and the civic curriculum of student government and community outreach are *currently* being learned (this will grant legitimacy, since we are already doing it, but didn't actually name what we were doing. Now we want to do it intentionally, and do it more consistently). Then we can develop additional—not too many!!!—learning opportunities in all three curricula. Have them reinforce one another, when possible. All around the themes of autonomy, connectedness and transcendence (or perhaps change the vocabulary ... too esoteric??) BUT ... Keep the meaning, the substance of those concepts.

6 Identify teachers and others who excel in connecting academics, student life, and civic curriculum, and have them work with less competent teachers to bring them up to level.

7 IMPORTANT ... Talk to the superintendent about this plan. Perhaps he might want us to pilot this. Stress this as a multiple year project, going to move one step at a time. Any foundations for some professional development and curriculum resources funds???

Our principal gets up from her desk, talking to herself. "That's enough for now. I'll fill this out, put in some timelines, may have enough for three years here. Talk to my advisory committee when I'm ready. See what the Super says."

Having explored what these imaginary uses of the book might look like, let us turn to an example in real life.

Beyond Imagining: Seeing It Happen

Early in 2005 I was fortunate to work as a visiting scholar at the Australian Catholic University (ACU) in Sydney in New South Wales. At the time I was developing the ideas on the moral character of learning (Starratt, 2005a) and the ethical leadership of schools (Starratt, 2005b). My time at ACU afforded opportunities to discuss these ideas in public lectures and in extended conversations with members of the educational leadership faculty there, many of whom were writing and lecturing on similar issues. Toward the end of my stay, a group of us drew up a skeletal outline of a possible initiative between the faculty at ACU and the Catholic schools in nearby diocesan schools systems. Plans were made to develop and implement an initiative that would involve teams from multiple schools over a two year period.

After my return home, discussions between ACU faculty and a team of diocesan school superintendents continued to develop the original plan and a design of a pilot project emerged, with the title, "Leaders Transforming Learning and Learners" (LTLL1). The pilot, involving nine elementary and high schools from four Catholic diocesan school systems, proved largely successful. Based on feedback from the pilot, a second initiative (LTLL2) was mounted involving eleven elementary and high schools from five Catholic school diocesan school systems. Both phases included a research component that was jointly shaped by university faculty, system administrators and representatives from schools who were involved. This research has revealed rather striking results, and provides for me examples of genuine efforts to cultivate ethical schooling.

At this point I turn the narrative over to Associate Professor Michael Bezzina of Australian Catholic University who has been involved with this initiative from the start.

The LTLL project

At the time when Professor Starratt was developing his ideas on ethical leadership, Catholic educators at ACU and in a number of Catholic school systems were wrestling with the question of how to best understand

and support the ways in which our schools could give expression to their explicit values base in both learning and leadership. The virtues of authenticity, responsibility, and presence (Starratt, 2004) seemed to us to hold promise as part of such an undertaking.

Extensive discussions among the stakeholders gave rise to a conceptual framework whose elements stood up to the test of implementation during the pilot study (LTLL1) and emerged in a slightly refined configuration for use in LTLL2—with a less linear, and more nuanced expression of the relationships among the elements.

The framework sought to make explicit the ways in which moral purpose might be seen to operate in schools, not simply as an abstraction, but through observable expressions of school life—particularly in the areas of learning and leadership. This moral purpose was seen as being an expression of the school's deepest hopes for its students—that they would be genuinely transformed learners. For this to happen, approaches to learning and to the ways in which leadership was expressed in the school would need to be informed not only by current understandings of best practice, but by the values and ethics already made explicit. Pivotal to the framework is the role of teacher as leader. The framework was grounded in the reality of schooling in a Reflection Guide that encouraged schools to consider what their school might look like if it were genuinely shaped by its sense of moral purpose.

The model used in LTLL2 appears in Figure 9.1.

The conceptual framework depicts the way in which the values and ethics shape the sense of the transformed learner (moral purpose) and influence the way both learning and leadership take place in the school, with teacher leadership as a critical element. This was then used by the partners to develop a program that would allow participant schools to engage in a process of refection and renewal, which in LTLL2 extended over two years. This included plenary gatherings, regional support, and in-school implementation of action based on reflection.

A set of criteria was developed for the selection of participant schools. The program was not conceived as a remedial initiative, but rather as one which might enable good schools to move to a new level in their operations. Schools were selected which were judged to best be able to capitalize on the opportunities provided by participation.

The five Catholic diocesan systems that were part of the project committed to support their schools both in terms of additional finance for the period of the initiative, and ongoing support from district personnel. Schools undertook to establish a team to lead their local initiative which included the principal, another senior member of staff, and one young teacher with no formal leadership role. All teams would gather together for

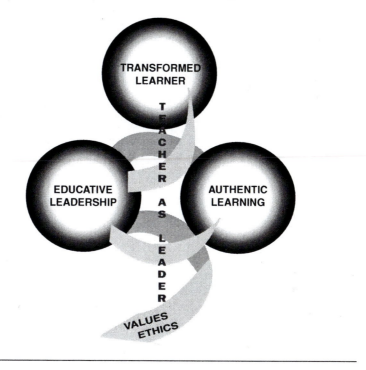

Figure 9.1 Model of the leaders transforming learning and learners project.

a full day plenary session six times in the course of the two years for input, sharing, and processing of new directions. The first plenary provided input on the conceptual framework as well as an opportunity to complete a detailed reflection guide that would shape the choice of a local initiative that could respond to areas of challenge or build on existing strengths. The next four sessions provided detailed input on the domains of the framework as well as skill development in the collection and use of evidence. A key element of the plenaries was that they provided opportunities for sharing among schools and refining of action plans in the light of input and feedback. Between plenaries, schools worked on the implementation of their plans, and particularly on engaging their colleagues in the process, with support from system personnel. The final plenary was a showcase of school initiatives, attended by senior staff of the various school systems.

Each school chose its own unique initiative, drawing on its reflection on the conceptual framework. Almost universally schools found themselves challenged by the extent to which student learning was authentic and genuinely transformative. The ways in which they chose to respond to this challenge, however, differed widely. A few examples will serve to illustrate this diversity. In pursuit of greater authenticity and increased student engagement, one high school took on project-based learning while another implemented an open space, cross-disciplinary learning. Three elementary schools took on the development of a set of core school values, a focus on boys' education and an early numeracy initiative respectively. No two of the eleven schools responded in the same way.

The ongoing feedback from schools and systems, the presentations at the final plenary, and the data from interviews with each school leadership team all indicated that something significant was happening in the schools. The data reported here was gathered at the end of the university's formal engagement with the schools, after two years. Despite the diversity of local initiatives, a pattern could be detected among the data that were gathered.

The reflective exercise focused the attention of school teams on the extent to which the learning going on in their schools was rich and significant, genuinely engaging their students in ways that had meaning for them, both now and into the future. They were frequently challenged by the gap they saw between their assumptions and/or rhetoric and their practice. They were often surprised by what they discovered through the process, throwing light on blind spots created by habit or neglect (Moberg, 2006).

This surprise expressed itself in the comments of individuals like this elementary teacher who observed that she had never really thought about moral purpose, either during her teacher education or during her first two years of teaching. She continued:

> I just knew I wanted to be a teacher, didn't think about why or anything. Learning about this transformational learning, I can't go back. I can't go back and teach any other way. If I go to another school I have no idea what I'm going to do because I now have to teach this way, I've had to change me personally.

This almost visceral response goes beyond compliance, or a superficial, short term change in technique. It reflects a deep and personal perspective that virtually demands a change—not as a matter of procedure, but as an ethical imperative, and not in response to a particular circumstance, but as a life-long commitment to principle.

Provoking this kind of response in individual teachers seems to have been necessary but not sufficient to bring about the kinds of change we saw in LTLL. A commitment to moral purpose on the part of one or two individuals was not enough to bring about change. Leaders in LTLL schools found that in the framework and the language it used, they had a vehicle that could be harnessed to sharing commitment to purpose (Bezzina, 2008). One high school principal expressed it this way:

For me also it gave literally a structure, if you like, for me mentally to hang a new principalship on because when I arrived we did a survey of what was needed and it was like this massive tower but it gave a real sense of making a manageable thing in terms of looking at the moral purpose. We used a lot of the terminology in the [Reflection Guide] document, in particular to help us.

While the secondary principal focused on the capacity of the framework and language to help make sense of complex situations, one primary principal emphasized the capacity of shared language to drive collaboration and shared purpose in his observation:

We've gone down a process with the staff over the last two years of first of all giving them the language of what moral purpose is all about. The biggest impact that I've seen as the principal is that the staff are now sitting together, they're developing work together and they're looking at what the reason behind doing the work is all about. So that whole sense of why are we doing it? What's the purpose of doing it? If it's not useful then why are we doing it?

This process of sensitizing individuals to the moral dimensions of an issue has resonances with the work of Tuana (2007) on moral literacy. The added dimension, and indeed the unique responsibility of the school leader is to go beyond the sensitizing of the individuals to develop a sense of commitment and agency in those individuals and beyond that, in the staff and parent communities. It is one thing to provide people with the time and space for sharing, but LTLL seems to have provided some missing ingredients—a significant agenda and a way of working with it. One high school principal described the process in action.

So I'm actually seeing a group of maybe eight people sitting down and saying, yeah, this is really good because it has this, this and this. Yeah, okay, I agree, I disagree and so on. So that has been really powerful as well. We think it probably wasn't until LTLL that that type of notion had even crossed a lot of people's minds. It certainly hadn't crossed mine.

The point at which moral purpose met practice in the minds of many of the LTLL teachers was in their attempts to engage students in learning which was more authentic. One elementary teacher put it this way:

We're thinking about what is really meaningful for the children, is going to make a difference for the 21st century child. Through that

process, everything we do, speaking from a teacher in the classroom, everything I do now, I think, what benefit is this going to be
to the children? How meaningful is this going to be in their life? Is
this really going to transform their learning?

In several schools, interestingly, the observation was made that LTLL
allowed them to make sense of, or to integrate existing initiatives by
addressing issues of purpose and authenticity rather than discrete sets of
mechanics and technique. In every school there were reported changes in
teacher attitudes and practice, and in student engagement and outcomes
(Bezzina and Burford, 2010).

With respect to teachers, there were widespread indications of changed
practice, most of which was a response to increased individualization:
consultation of students, curriculum integration, curriculum differentiation, and team teaching. There was an increased use of evidence to shape
teaching. One school reported a drop by 65 percent in the amount of
photocopying being done by teachers—usually in the form of worksheets
for students. Another noted an increase in teachers volunteering time for
extra curricular activities. Attitudinal change among staff was widespread,
with the following comment from one elementary school being typical: "It
is everyone's responsibility to care for each student. Staff now realize this
and accept it."

One of the interesting dynamics was the challenge to the way in which
teachers conceptualize their approach to material. This extended quotation from one elementary school highlights the way in which teachers are
learners too in the process.

We kept thinking we've got these nice units of work and they're
taught quite well, there are a bunch of activities that lead to an end
and the kids are very happy to sit there and learn and regurgitate
back what they need to show the teacher that they understand, but
what we were missing from these units of work was the so what.
Okay they can collect knowledge and collect facts about the environment or Antarctica or the government but at the end of if you
need to say now I know this knowledge where do I go (with it)?

That's a hard one for teachers too because to ask the right questions can be really difficult and to work with that complacency can
be really difficult. (LTLL has led to) implementing programs of
learning where they actually challenge the teachers initially: so why
would you want them to think like this … what are you looking for
in the unit and what kind of things can you do? Have you thought
about this? Very often its teachers going, "Oh no I haven't thought
about that." So that's been really worthwhile too.

Beyond the classroom, schools reported increased levels of teacher leadership and empowerment, as in the case of this school:

> It happened organically, it didn't happen because we said, okay, now you're teacher leaders. It just flowed. It just kind of happened. All of a sudden these people were stepping up and taking on leadership roles.

In this particular case, one of the teachers to emerge as significant leader was in only her second year of teaching. For this kind of thing to be able to happen, there needs to be a climate of trust. One of the battles of leaders is to build this climate—a process that takes time. The following quotation from an elementary school teacher gives a sense of how important this is.

> People trust one another. Not completely everyone but they're getting there. It's that you're not going to judge me, you're going to help me. That's huge, it's really big.

In the case of students, several schools, which had chosen an academic focus, reported significant increases in standardized testing outcomes. Others indicated a drop-off in behavioral referrals, or an increase in student satisfaction ratings, or higher levels of student engagement. One high school spoke about increasing proactivity among its students, with "evidence that students are beginning to drive change in the school, and ... have become aware of their voice being heard." At the same time, that school reported that more students were concerned about their learning and more discerning about quality learning. One high school surveyed students and identified 75 percent of students who reported that they had gained new learning skills.

Many teachers commented on the increasing sophistication of the ways in which students engaged with learning. One elementary teacher said:

> I think they're getting so used to reflecting and asking themselves why are we learning it that they do see the value of everything that you learn because they do have that curiosity now: "So how is this going to change my life?"

Another school reported on the process they used in which students wrote to their local member of parliament about a traffic issue—a rich, grounded, and multidimensional exercise which allowed students to engage as citizens in real issues using learning they had gained in school.

One might be tempted to ask whether this approach to learning is beyond younger students. In one case at least, that proved not to be the case. Two teachers excitedly reported their experience with a kindergarten class.

A: If you want an anecdote, kindergarten do a unit of work on animals. I think previously it was a nice unit where they classified animals into mammals and marsupials and labeled them in the zoo and built a little enclosure. These kids now get to the third question which is "How can we help protect animals in our environment or in the world environment?"—and they start researching things like—what was it about the mobile [cell] phones?

B: The coltan, the kindergartens told me that coltan, which is a metal in mobile phones, is being mined in an area where gorillas live. So they did a recycling drive so that the coltan wasn't being mined and the gorillas ...

This is a good example of the way in which this deeper, richer approach to learning impacts on all those who come in contact with it. These teachers had to research for themselves what coltan was. I confess that I had to do the same! It is the East African name for the ore from which tantalum (a key element of cell phone batteries) is extracted.

At this point, Professor Starratt resumes the narrative.

Concluding Comments

From this necessarily brief description of this Australian initiative (which was not labeled "Cultivating an Ethical School," but which tacitly involved the ten elements described in the previous chapter), we can begin to get a sense of the spirit behind the theme of this book. The quotations from principals and teachers and the examples they cite indicate that a significant transformation of the work of the school is in the making. That transformation involves some structural changes in the ways schools organize the work, some advances in the technical side of teachers pedagogy and curriculum redesign, some new sense of leadership density among teachers, but more than anything, the transformation being enacted has been energized by looking deeply at the moral purpose and the moral outcomes of learning and teaching. That transformation has involved a deepening or recapturing of the very identity of the learners as learners, the identity of the teachers as teachers, and the identity of the local school as involved in meaningful, transforming work. For both teachers and students, their work now involves a significant living out of their daily lives, being active in their daily lives in creating that personal, significant meaning, instead of passively accepting the routines of work designed by someone else.

Were we to rate each school and the process they are engaging (a process still very much incomplete) using the ten elements as a template, we could find an implicit involvement with and enactment of each of the elements—but differently in each school, both in depth and integration with the other elements.

Ten Elements Implicitly or Explicitly Present in the LTLL Process

- A clear mission statement that will provide a compass for the activities, operations, and policies of the school. **Mostly explicit, but often ignored in practice prior to LTLL.**
- A foundation in both general and professional ethical perspectives. **Focus on ethics of authenticity in the work and the results of the work.**
- A foundation in a theory of human development. **Implicit (connecting to student growing sense of identity and moral purpose to his/her life, and teachers recapturing their identity as a teacher with a moral purpose).**
- A foundation in a learning theory that will guide the pedagogy of the school. **Implicit: Authentic learning connects the learner to the trajectory of her/his life.**
- An academic, social, and civic curriculum that is consistent with the school's theory of learning. **Explicit: Each school engaged in making some part of their curriculum authentic.**
- Teachers and administrators who are committed to the work of such a school. **Explicit: Principals' and teacher leaders' commitment quite vocal.**
- Working relationships with the home and the local community. **Explicit in some schools, implicit in others depending on the type of initiative selected.**
- Ethical organizational policies, structures, and procedures. **Explicit in some; others beginning to engage.**
- An ethical school culture. **All schools moving toward an explicit culture of moral purpose.**
- Ethical outcomes. **All schools explicitly mention impact of moral purpose on students' and teachers' behavior, but the amount of evidence varied from school to school.**

Obviously, Professor Bezzina and I see LTLL as a work in progress, as the above assessment indicates. At the same time there are lessons to be learned about the approach to transforming the schooling process through a focus on the moral purpose embedded in the teaching learning process.

One distinguishing feature of LTLL is that it involved teams from several schools from different school districts. Though each school had considerable latitude to focus on a particular area as the starting point for transforming the learning process, every school was further encouraged and energized by hearing the progress reports of the other participating schools. Being part of a two year launching process also provided time for each school team to meet, discuss, experiment, and assess their initial and ongoing efforts at implementation. Altogether the structural supports and positive critique encouraged a dynamic of internal accountability in each school.

Another distinguishing reason for the success of LTLL has been the trust of the facilitators to encourage each school to address its own sense of what it needed to do in the light of its sense of itself as an educating community. That work to be sure, will continue to play out over successive years.

This overview of the LTLL project helps us to see the long term commitment necessary to produce satisfying results in cultivating an ethical school.

CHAPTER 10

The Complexity of Ethical Living and Learning

Cultivating an ethical school is never a finished task, just as living an ethical life is never a final accomplishment. Much of ethical experience is complex and saturated with ambiguity. To be sure, many ethical choices are simple and straightforward. Should I walk out of the store without paying for the merchandise? Should I falsely accuse someone of breaking the window, when I am the one who broke it? Usually, the answers to these ethical questions pose no problems. But other situations may not be so clear. If we put ourselves in a student's place, we would have to struggle with many of their questions. How should I treat a bully who is picking on my older brother? How should I respond to the demands of a drunken parent? How should I respond to a police officer who uses an ethnic slur when addressing me? How do I respond to my best friend who wants to copy my homework? How do I respond when my classmates are scapegoating a student I don't like? How do I respond to a reckless driver who pulls out of a side street just in front of me, without even slowing down at the stop sign? How do I respond to another person who shoves me against the lockers in the school corridor? How do I respond when I see some of my friends making fun of a handicapped person? For many young people, the complexities of social life—when their own identities are only in the process of being formed, and their loyalties uncertain—leave them morally conflicted or uncertain. Not a few adults face similar uncertainties as they confront ethical choices.

It is relatively easy to speak in generalities of autonomy, connectedness, and transcendence, as well as justice, caring, and critique. In lived experience, however, circumstances often pose two or three apparently valid interpretations of what comprises autonomy, connectedness and transcendence. In other circumstances, our connectedness may be to two people to whom we owe allegiance, but only one of whom can be served by our decision, while the other is harmed by our decision.

In any given ethical decision we often find layers of motives, some of which are self-serving, some of which are more altruistic. Most situations in our lives involve ambiguities, ironies, and paradoxes. We are seldom all aligned in one direction toward virtue. Self-deception and rationalization constantly intrude, often at a subliminal level that avoids detection until someone else points it out to us. For persons of integrity, living ethically usually involves struggle and conflict; even the virtuous have their moments of weariness and discouragement, when the easy way out is chosen over the more ethically "correct" response.

Cultivating an ethical school will demand that teachers always communicate that they care about the moral tone of the school community. That caring, however, will always have to be mixed with sensitivity to the difficulty that even mature adults, let alone children and adolescents, have with consistently living an ethical life. Teachers will have to set limits, but the limits should be imposed with love and compassion. The ethical school will exhibit "tough love" at times; at other times it will exhibit unconditional love; it should teach students how to forgive themselves and each other. It should also acknowledge that ethical values are expressed in a variety of ways, and be aware that sometimes students will express their values in unpredictable and unconventional ways. The ethical school, while standing for ethical values, also has to avoid the self-righteousness of the ethical know-it-all, admitting that in some instances certainty eludes us all.

For the ethical school to succeed, all the members will need constantly to remind themselves that this is a human enterprise. As such, they should expect mistakes and imperfections. They will have to remind themselves that human beings are flawed and inconsistent, that despite their best intentions, self-interest will creep in to even the most altruistic of enterprises. The effort has to be entered upon with a sense of humility and sustained with a sense of compassion; otherwise it will defeat itself by expecting too much and by becoming a prisoner of its unrealistic expectations. The community will have to remind itself constantly that one learns to become ethical perhaps more often by learning from failures than by celebrating successes.

Summary

Throughout this book I have insisted on the cultivating of ethical character of the educating process and the need for creating multiple supports and expressions of its ethical character. Now, in this last chapter, am I allowing myself to be defeated by doubts as to its feasibility? To think so would be a misreading of the argument of this chapter. I believe that educators must continuously struggle to cultivate an ethical school; that struggle is integral to any process that deserves the name of education. In our exploration of a rationale and a process for cultivating an ethical school it is natural that high expectations would arise. Without backing down from those high expectations, it is important to realize that the experience of the ethical community will always involve the comedy and tragedy of the human situation.

Ethical education is not a simple training in the predisposition to be ethical, the lessons of which, once learned, guarantee an ethical adulthood. Ethical education is a lifelong education. It takes place simultaneously with our efforts to be human. We learn to be human in the *struggle* for integrity. Virtue is not something we achieve and then continue to possess. Virtue is always out in front of us to be achieved; it involves a perpetual doing. The human person is always incomplete. In a sense we do not create ourselves, we do ourselves. We do not make "good works"; we do good. We can't lay it out ahead of time. We can't say, now that I have developed and possess this virtue, I know how to act in this or that circumstance, in advance. The virtuous act must be continuously sought and improvised (Meilaender, 1984).

Since ethical education is a life-long experience, it should begin in school so that the process of ethical learning can become more intentionally reflective and its lessons more clearly learned. Paradoxically, we learn what it is to be human as well when we *fail* as when we succeed. In failure, we learn the hard lesson of our limits and the ambivalence of our motives, and the wonderful lesson of being forgiven by our fellows. We learn through failure the lesson of compassion, compassion for ourselves and compassion for our brothers and sisters. We discover the emptiness of a self-centered life, and the richness of a life whose connections sustain us even in our failures. In the pursuit and occasional achievement of some virtuous activity, we discover the quiet joy of enhancing someone else's life, the satisfaction of easing someone else's pain, the surprising pleasure when our honoring a relationship is acknowledged, the paradoxical fulfillment of ourselves when we give away ourselves. The learning is in the striving, not simply of the individual but in experiencing the striving of the community, where we gain our humanity in interaction with other humans who are struggling with all the heroic ambiguities of the human condition. A perfect ethical community would probably bore us to tears; we would not recognize it as a human community. A human community is a community that expresses the full range of the journey toward its fulfillment; in short a divine comedy. In school, we learn that our life, collectively and individually, is a divine comedy, but that the direction it takes is our responsibility.

Cultivating an ethical school, then, calls for great courage, a modicum of intelligence, lots of humility, humor, and compassion, and an unyielding hope in the endurance and heroism of human beings. It is a dream worthy of educators.

Notes

1 I am indebted to the late Professor Hedley Beare, a highly influential and esteemed educator in Australia, for many of the insights and concerns about the changing contexts of schooling internationally, to be found in his book *Creating the future school*, New York & London: Routledge/Falmer (2001). I have also been influenced by the work of Professor Yin Cheong Chen of the Hong Kong Institute of Education, *New paradigm for re-engineering education: Globalization, localization and individualization,* Dordrecht: Springer (2005). His work brings together much of the recent educational research and thinking in Pacific Rim countries that offers fruitful suggestions for Western educators as well.

2 In the development of the ideas of this chapter, I have been helped by Ernest Becker's (1968) brilliant treatment of the ethical person in his *The structure of evil* (especially ch. 11), New York: The Free Press. His work is a synthesis of earlier works by Martin Buber, Max Scheler, John Dewey, Josiah Royce, Max Weber, Ralph Waldo Emerson, and others. Émile Durkheim (1961), of course, has written the classic exposition on the centrality of autonomy and relationships to all moral actions in his book, *Moral education* (trans. by E.K. Wilson & H. Schnurer), New York: The Free Press. I also found Thomas Green's treatment of moral education enormously appealing, but have chosen to focus on these three basic qualities rather than on his "five voices of conscience," which I believe can easily be related to my trilogy. See Green, T.F. (1985) The formation of conscience in an age of technology, *The American Journal of Education,* 93, (1), pp. 1–38. More recently, Martha Nussbaum's book, *Creating capabilities: The human development approach,* Cambridge, MA: Belknap Press, 2011, echoes the basic thrust of this chapter. Criticizing the exclusive measure of a nation's wealth as its GNP, Nussbaum looks, rather, at a nation's wealth in terms of the human capabilities it nurtures and supports, particularly through the educational opportunities it provides for its people. Likewise, I would contend that rather than using the exclusive measure of AYP (Annual Yearly Progress on state or national tests), states should also evaluate their success at growing their young citizens' capabilities to live humanly fulfilling, ethically responsible, and productive civic lives through their educational system.

3 This chapter is a substantial rewrite of an earlier publication, Building an ethical school: A theory for practice in educational administration. *Educational Administration Quarterly,* 27(2), 1991, 185–202.

4 This analysis of Erik Erikson's work has been enormously facilitated by the work of James Cote and Charles Levine in their book, *Identity formation, agency, and culture: A social*

psychological synthesis (Mahwah, NJ: Lawrence Erlbaum, 2002). This chapter incorporates and develops a recent commentary on Erikson's work (Starratt, 2011).

5 This section is adapted from an earlier essay published as Grounding moral educational leadership in the morality of teaching and learning in *Leading and Managing,* 4(4), pp. 243–255, and from similar treatment in Thomas J. Sergiovanni and Robert J. Starratt, *Supervision: A Redefinition,* McGraw-Hill (2007), pp. 72–80.

References

Adams, P. (2004). Supporting teachers' professional development. In P.E. Holland (Ed.), *Beyond measure: Neglected elements of accountability* (pp. 101–132). Larchmont, NY: Eye on Education.

Adorno, T.W. (1973). *Negative dialectics*. New York: Seabury Press.

Andrzejewski, J., Baltodano, M.P., & Symcox, L. (2009). Social justice, peace, and environmental education. In J. Andrzejewski, M.P. Baltodano, & L. Symcox (Eds.), *Social justice, peace, and environmental education: Transformative standards* (pp. 1–16). New York: Routledge.

Apple, M. (2004). *Ideology and curriculum* (3rd ed.). New York: Routledge.

Applebee, A.N. (1996). *Curriculum as conversation*. Chicago: University of Chicago Press.

Augros, R.M. & Stanciu, G.N. (1987). *The new biology: Discovering the wisdom in nature*. Boston: New Science Library.

Barry, B. (1973). *A liberal theory of justice: A critical examination of the principal doctrines in a theory of justice by John Rawls*. Oxford, UK: Clarendon Press.

Bart, W. (1977). Piagetian cognitive theory and adult education. Paper presented at the Adult Education Research Conference, University of Minnesota, Minneapolis, MN.

Bateson, G. (1979a). *Mind and nature: A necessary unity*. New York: E.P. Dutton.

Bateson, G. (1979b). *Steps to an ecology of mind*. New York: Ballantine Books.

Bauman, Z. (1997). *Postmodernity and its discontents*. New York: New York University Press.

Beare, H. (2001). *Creating the future school*. New York & London: Routledge/Falmer.

Beck, U. (2006). *The cosmopolitan vision*. Cambridge: Polity Press.

Beck, U. (2009). *World at risk*. Trans. by Ciaran Cronin. Cambridge: Polity Press.

Becker, E. (1968). *The structure of evil*. New York: The Free Press.

Becker, E. (1971). *The birth and death of meaning* (2nd ed.). New York: The Free Press.

Belenky, M.F., Clinchy, B.M., Goldberg, N.R., & Tarule, J.M. (1986). *Women's ways of knowing: The development of self, voice, and mind*. New York: Basic Books.

Bellah, R.N., Madsen, R., Sullivan, W.M., Swidler, A., & Tipton, S.M. (1985). *Habits of the heart: Individualism and commitment in American life*. Berkeley, CA: University of California Press.

Bezzina, M. (2008). We do make a difference: Shared moral purpose and shared leadership in the pursuit of learning. *Leading and Managing, 14*(1), 38–59.

Bezzina, M. & Burford, C. (2010). Leaders transforming learning and learners: An Australian innovation in leadership, learning and moral purpose. In A.H. Normore (Ed.), *Global perspectives on educational leadership reform: The development and preparation of leaders of learning and learners of leadership* (Vol. 11, pp. 201–211). Bingley, UK: Emerald.

Blasi, A. (1984). Moral identity: Its role in moral functioning. In W.M. Kurtines & J.L. Gewirtz (Eds.), *Morality, moral behavior and moral development* (pp. 128–139). New York: Wiley.

Block, J.E. (2002). *A nation of agents: The American path to a modern self and society.* Cambridge, MA: Belknap Press of Harvard University Press.

Bohn, D. (1995). *Wholeness and the intricate order.* London: Routledge.

Bonnet, M. & Cuypers, S. (2003). Autonomy and authenticity in education. In N. Blake, P. Smeyers, R. Smith, & P. Standish (Eds.), *The Blackwell guide to the philosophy of education* (pp. 326–340). Oxford: Blackwell.

Bowers, C.A. (1987). *Elements of a post liberal theory of education.* New York: Teachers College Press.

Bowers, C.A. (2002). Toward a cultural and ecological understanding of curriculum. In W.E. Doll, Jr. & N. Gough (Eds.), *Curriculum visions* (pp. 75–85). New York: Peter Lang.

Bradley, J. (2009). *The imperial cruise: A secret history of empire and war.* New York: Back Bay Publishing/Little, Brown and Company.

Bruner, J. (1987). The transactional self. In J. Bruner & H. Haste (Eds.), *Making sense: The child's construction of the world* (pp. 81–96). New York: Methuen.

Bruner, J. (1990). *Acts of meaning.* Cambridge, MA: Harvard University Press.

Bryk, A. & Schneider, B. (2004). *Trust in schools: A core resource for improvement.* New York: Russell Sage Foundation.

Buber, M. (1955). *Between man and man.* Boston: Beacon Press.

Buber, M. (1958). *I and thou* (2nd ed.). Trans by R.G. Smith. New York: Scribners.

Butts, R.F. (1988). The moral imperative for American schools: … "Inflame the civic temper…". *American Journal of Education*, 96, 162–194.

Capra, F. (1982). *The turning point: Science, society and culture.* New York: Bantam Books.

Chadorow, N. (1978). *The reproduction of mothering.* London: University of California Press.

Chadorow, N. (1989). *Feminism and psychoanalytic theory.* New Haven, CT: Yale University Press.

Chatwin, B. (1987). *Songlines.* New York: Penguin Books.

Cheng, Y.C. (2005). *New paradigm for re-engineering education: Globalization, localization, and individualization.* Dordrecht, NE: Springer.

Christensen, L. (2009). *Teaching for joy and justice.* Milwaukee, WI: Rethinking Schools Publications.

Colby, A. & Damon, W. (1992). *Some do care: Contemporary lives of moral commitment.* New York: Maxwell Macmillan.

Conn, W.E. (1977). Erik Erikson: The ethical orientation, conscience, and the Golden Rule. *Journal of Religious Education*, 5(2), 249–266.

Cote, J. & Levine, C. (2002). *Identity formation, agency, and culture: A social psychological synthesis.* Mahwah, NJ: Lawrence Erlbaum.

Damon, W. (1984). Self-understanding and moral development from childhood to adolescence. In W.M. Kurtines & J.L. Giwertz (Eds.). *Morality, moral behavior and moral development* (pp. 109–127). New York: Wiley.

Davidson, P. & Youniss, J. (1995). Moral development and social construction. In W.M. Kurtines & J.L. Gewirtz (Eds.), *Moral development: An introduction* (pp. 289–310). Needham Heights, MA: Allyn & Bacon.

Delors, J., Al Mufti, I., Amagi, A., Carneiro, R., Chung, F. Geremek, B. et al. (1996). *Learning: The treasure within—Report to UNESCO of the International Commission on Education for the Twenty-first Century.* Paris: United Nations Educational, Scientific, and Cultural Organization.

Dewey, J. (1916). *Democracy and education: An introduction to the philosophy of education.* New York: Macmillan.

Dewey, J. (1927). *The public and its problems.* New York: Henry Holt Company.

Drummond, M.J. (2001). Children yesterday, today, and tomorrow. In J. Collins & D. Cook

(Eds.), *Understanding learning: Influences and outcomes* (pp. 84–95). London: Paul Chapman and Open University Press.

Durkheim, E. (1961). *Moral education*. Trans. by E.K. Wilson & H. Schnurer. New York: Free Press.

Egan, K. (1990*). Romantic understanding: The development of rationality and imagination, ages 8–15*. New York: Routledge.

Egan, K. (1997). *The educated mind: How cognitive tools shape our understanding*. Chicago: University of Chicago Press.

Egan, K. (1999). *Children's minds, talking rabbits & clockwork oranges: Essays on education*. New York: Teachers College Press.

Eiseley, L. (1957). *The immense journey*. New York: Vantage Books.

Eiseley, L. (1962). *The mind as nature*. New York: Charles Scribner's Sons.

Erikson, E.H. (1957). Identity and the life cycle. *Psychological Issues, 1*(1), 18–171.

Erikson, E.H. (1963). *Childhood and society* (2nd ed.). New York: W.W. Norton.

Erikson, E.H. (1964). *Insight and responsibility*. New York: W.W. Norton.

Erikson, E.H. (1968). *Identity: Youth and crisis*. New York: W.W. Norton.

Erikson, E.H. (1974) *Dimensions of a new identity*. New York: W.W. Norton.

Erikson, E.H. (1980). *Identity and the life cycle*. New York: W.W Norton.

Ernst, S. (1997) Mothers and daughters in a changing world. In W. Hollway & B. Featherstone (Eds.), *Mothering and ambivalence* (pp. 80–88). London: Routledge.

Fisher, B. & Tronto, J. (1990). Towards a feminist theory of caring. In E.K. Abel & M. Nelson (Eds.), *Circle of care: Work and identity in women's lives* (pp. 35–62). Albany, NY: State University of New York Press.

Fiske, S.T. & Taylor, S.E. (1991). *Social cognition* (2nd ed.). New York: McGraw-Hill.

Freire, P. (1970). *Pedagogy of the oppressed*. Trans. by Myra Bergman Ramos. New York: Herder and Herder.

Fromm, E. (1956). *The art of loving*. New York: Harpers.

Fuller, F.W. (2004). *Somebodies and nobodies: Overcoming the abuse of rank*. Gabriola Island, CA: New Society Publishers.

Gibbs, J. (1995). The cognitive developmental perspective. In W.M. Kurtines & J.L. Gewirtz (Eds.), *Moral development: An introduction* (pp. 27–48). Needham Heights, MA: Allyn & Bacon.

Gilligan, C. (1982). *In a different voice: Psychological theory and women's development*. Cambridge, MA: Harvard University Press.

Goffman, E. (1959). *The presentation of the self in everyday life*. Garden City, NY: Doubleday.

Green, T.F. (1985). The formation of conscience in an age of technology. *American Journal of Education*, 93 (1), pp. 1–38.

Griffin, D.R. (Ed.) (1990). *Sacred interconnections: Post-modern spirituality, political economy and art*. Albany, NY: State University of New York Press.

Habermas, J. (1971). *Knowledge and human interests*. Trans. by Jeremy Shapiro. Boston: Beacon Press.

Habermas, J. (1973). *Legitimation crisis*. Boston: Beacon Press.

Habermas, J. (2006). *The divided West*. Trans. by Ciaran Cronin. Cambridge: Polity Press.

Hallowell, E.M. (1999). *Connect*. New York: Pantheon Books.

Hargreaves, A. & Fink, D. (2006). *Sustainable leadership*. San Francisco: Jossey-Bass.

Hoare, C.H. (2002). *Erikson on development in adulthood*. New York: Oxford University Press.

Hogan, P. (2010). *The new significance of learning: Imagination's heartwork*. New York and London: Routledge.

Hollway, W. (2006). *The capacity to care: Gender and ethical subjectivity*. London: Routledge.

Hollway, W. & Featherstone, B. (Eds.) (1997). *Mothering and ambivalence*. London: Routledge.

Horkheimer, M. (1985). *Critique of instrumental reason: Lectures and essays since the end of World War II*. Trans by Matthew J. O'Connell et al. New York: Continuum.

Horsman, R. (1981). *Race and manifest destiny: The origins of American racial Anglo-Saxonism.* Cambridge, MA: Harvard University Press.

Johnson, R. (1983). *He: Understanding masculine psychology.* San Francisco: Harper & Row.

Jordan, J. et al. (1991). *Women's growth in connection: Writings from the Stone Center.* New York: Guilford Press.

Judis, J.B. (2004). *The folly of empire: What George W. Bush could learn from Teddy Roosevelt and Woodrow Wilson.* New York: Lisa Drew/Scribners.

Kelcourse, F.B. (2004). *Human development and faith: Life-cycle stages of body, mind, and soul.* St. Louis, MO: Chalice Press.

Knowles, R.T. (1986). *Human Development and human possibility: Erikson in the light of Heidegger.* Lanham, MD: University Press of America.

Kohlberg, L. (1981). *The philosophy of moral development: Moral stages and the idea of justice.* San Francisco: Harper & Row.

Kurtines, W.M. & Gewirtz, J.L. (1995). Moral development: An introduction and overview. In W.M. Kurtines & J. L. Gewirtz (Eds.), *Moral development: An introduction* (pp. 1–15). Needham Heights, MA: Allyn & Bacon.

Langlois, L. & Lapointe, C. (2004). Ethical leadership in linguistic minority settings: Adding new colors to the patchwork. Paper delivered at the University Council of Educational Administration (UCEA) Conference, Montreal, November 11–13.

Langlois, L. & Lapointe, C. (2010) Can ethics be learned? Results from a three-year action research project. *Journal of Educational Administration, 48*(2), 147–163.

Lovelock, J. (1995). *Gaia: A new look at life on earth.* Oxford: Oxford University Press.

McCarthy, E.D. (1996*). Knowledge as culture: The new sociology of knowledge.* London: Routledge.

Macdonald, J.B. (1971). A vision of a humane school. In J.G. Saylor & J.L. Smith (Eds.), *Barriers to humanness in the high school* (pp. 2–20). Washington, DC: Association of Supervision and Curriculum Development.

Macintyre, A. (1981). *After virtue.* Notre Dame, IN: University of Notre Dame Press.

McKibben, W. (2010). *Earth: Making a life on a tough new planet.* New York: Time Books.

Macpherson, C.B. (1962). *The political theory of possessive individualism: Hobbes to Locke.* London: Oxford University Press.

Macy, J. (1990). The ecological self: Postmodern ground for right action. In Griffin, D.R. (Ed.), *Sacred interconnections: Post-modern spirituality, political economy and art,* Albany, NY: State University of New York Press. pp. 35–48.

Marcuse, H. (1966). *One-dimensional man: Studies in the ideology of advanced industrial society.* Boston: Beacon Press.

Mason, M. (2005). *The new accountability: Responsibility across borders.* London: Earthscan.

Mawhinney, H.B. (2004) Deliberative democracy in imagined communities: How the power geometry of globalization shapes local leadership praxis, *Educational Administration Quarterly 40*, 192–221.

Meilaender, G.C. (1984). *The theory and practice of virtue.* Notre Dame, IN: University of Notre Dame Press.

Mitchell, S.A. (2000). *Relationality: From attachment to intersubjectivity.* Hillsdale, NJ: Analytic Press.

Moberg, D.J. (2006). Ethics blind spots in organizations: How systematic errors in person perception undermine moral agency. *Organization Studies, 27,* 413–428.

Morrison, B. (2007). Schools and restorative justice. In G. Johnstone & D.W. Van Ness (Eds.), *Handbook of restorative justice.* Devon: Willan Publishers.

Mumford, L. (1964). The forces of life. In P. Goodman (Ed.), *Seeds of liberation* (pp. 498–507). New York: George Braziller.

Nixon, J., Martin, J., McKeown, P. & Ranson, S. (1996). *Encouraging learning: Towards a theory of the learning school.* London: Open University Press.

Noddings, N. (1984). *Caring: A feminine approach to ethics and moral education.* Berkeley, CA: University of California Press.

Noddings, N. (1992). *The challenge to care in schools: An alternative approach to education*. New York: Teachers College Press.

Nucci, L. (2008). Social cognitive domain theory and moral education. In L.P. Nucci & D. Narvaez (Eds.), *Handbook of moral and character education* (pp. 291–309). New York: Routledge.

Nussbaum, M. (1990). Transcending humanity. *Love's knowledge: Essays on philosophy and literature* (pp. 365–391). New York: Oxford University Press.

Nussbaum, M. (2011). *Creating capabilities: The human development approach*. Cambridge, MA: Belknap Press.

Pearson, C. (1986). *The hero within us: Six archetypes we live by*. San Francisco: Harper & Row.

Piaget, J. (1971). The theory of stages in cognitive development. In D.R Green, M.P. Ford & G.B. Flamer (Eds.), *Measurement and Piaget* (pp. 1–11). New York: McGraw-Hill.

Piaget, J. (1975). *The development of thought: Equilibration of cognitive structure*. New York: Viking Press.

Polanyi, M. (1966). *The tacit dimension*. Garden City, NY: Doubleday.

Prigogene, I. & Stengers, I. (1984). *Order out of chaos: Man's new dialogue with nature*. New York: Bantam Books.

Raphael, R. (1988). *The men from the boys: Rites of passage in male America*. Lincoln, NE: University of Nebraska Press.

Rawls, J. (1971) *A theory of justice*. Cambridge, MA: Belknap Press of Harvard University Press.

Reay, D. & William, D. (2001). "I'll be a nothing": Structure, agency, and the construction of identity through assessment. In J. Collins & D. Cook (Eds.), *Understanding learning: Influences and outcomes* (pp. 149–161). London: Paul Chapman Publishers and Open University Press.

Rest, J., Narvaez, D., Bebeau, M.J., & Thoma, S.J. (1999). *Postconventional moral thinking: A Neo-Kohlbergian approach*. Mahwah, NJ: Lawrence Erlbaum.

Riesman, D. (1950). *The lonely crowd*. New Haven, CT: Yale University Press.

Riestenberg, N. (n.d.). Applying the framework: Positive youth development and restorative practices: http://f.p.enter.net/restorativepractices/beth06_riestenberg.pdf. Accessed 6/27/2011.

Roazen, P. (1997). *Erik Erikson: The power and limits of a vision*. Northvale, NJ: Jason Aronson.

Ruckriem, G. (1999). The crisis of knowledge. In M. Hedegaard & J. Lompscher (Eds.), *Learning activity and development* (pp. 93–122). Oxford: Aarhus University Press.

Sarason, S.B. (2004). *And what do you mean by learning?* Portsmouth, NH: Heinemann.

Scheler, M. (1957). *The nature of sympathy*. London: Routledge & Kegan Paul.

Seilstad, G.A. (1989). *At the heart of the web: The inevitable genesis of intelligent life*. New York: Harcourt Brace.

Sergiovanni, T.J. (1992). *The moral dimensions of leadership*. San Francisco: Jossey-Bass.

Sergiovanni, T.J. (2001). *The principalship: A reflective practice perspective*. Boston: Allyn & Bacon.

Sergiovanni, T.J. & Starratt, R.J. (1998). *Supervision: A redefinition*. New York: McGraw-Hill.

Shapiro, J.P. & Stefkovich, J.A. (2001). *Ethical leadership and decision making in education: Applying theoretical perspectives to complex dilemmas*. Mahwah, NJ: Lawrence Erlbaum.

Shils, E. (1981). *Tradition*. Chicago: University of Chicago Press.

Shultz, J.S. & Cook-Sather, A. (2001). *In our own words: Students' perspectives on school*. Lanham, MD: Rowan & Littlefield.

Sichtermann, B. (1986). *Femininity: The politics of the personal*. Trans. by John Whitlam. Minneapolis, MN: University of Minnesota Press.

Sidorkin, A.M. (2002). *Learning relations*. New York: Peter Lang.

Sizer, T.R. (1996). *Horace's hope*. Boston: Houghton Mifflin.

Skeggs, B. (1997). *Formations of class and gender*. London: Sage.

Smyth, J., Angus, L., Down, B., & McInerney, P. (2009). *Activist and social critical school and community renewal: Social justice in exploitative times*. Rotterdam: Sense Publishers.

Sokolowski, R. (1991). The fiduciary relationship and the nature of professions. In E.D. Pellegrino,

R.M. Veatch, & J.P. Langan (Eds.), *Ethics, trust, and the professions* (pp. 23–39). Washington, DC: Georgetown University Press.

Spring, J. (2010). *Deculturalization and the struggle for equality: A brief history of the education of dominated cultures in the United States* (6th ed.). Boston: McGraw Hill.

Sprinthall, N.A. and Theis-Sprinthall, L. (1983). The teacher as adult learner: A cognitive-developmental view. In G. Griffin (Ed.), *Staff development*. Eighty Second Yearbook of the National Society for the Study of Education, Part II, pp. 13–35. Chicago: University of Chicago Press.

Stern, N. (2007). *The economics of climate change: The Stern review*. Cambridge: Cambridge University Press.

Starratt, R.J. (1969). The individual and the educated imagination: An essay in curriculum theory. Unpublished doctoral dissertation, Department of Educational Administration, University of Illinois, Champaign/Urbana, IL.

Starratt, R.J. (1989). Knowing at the level of sympathy: A curriculum challenge. *Journal of curriculum and supervision, 4*(3), 271.

Starratt, R.J. (1991). Building an ethical school: A theory for practice in educational leadership. *Educational Administration Quarterly, 27*(2), 185–202.

Starratt, R.J. (1994). *Building an Ethical School*. London: Falmer Press.

Starratt, R.J. (2004). *Ethical leadership*. San Francisco: Jossey-Bass.

Starratt, R.J. (2005a). Cultivating the moral character of learning and teaching: A neglected dimension of educational leadership. *School Leadership and Management 25*(4), 399–411.

Starratt, R.J. (2005b) Ethical leadership. In B. Davies (Ed.), *The essentials of school leadership* (pp. 61–74). London: Sage.

Starratt, R.J. (2007). Leading a community of learners: Learning to be moral by engaging the morality of learning. *Educational Management, Administration and Leadership 35*(2), 165–183.

Starratt, R.J. (2009). Dewey's democracy and education revisited: A continuing leadership agenda. In P.M. Jenlink (Ed.), *Dewey's democracy and education revisited: Contemporary discourses for democratic education and leadership* (pp. 52–70). New York: Rowman & Littlefield.

Starratt, Robert J. (2010). The moral character of academic learning: Challenging the exclusivity of the reigning paradigm of school learning. In A. Hargreaves, A. Lieberman, M. Fullan, & D. Hopkins (Eds.), *Second International Handbook of Educational Change* (pp. 631–645). London/New York: Springer.

Starratt, R.J. (2011). *Refocusing school leadership: Foregrounding human development throughout the work of the school*. New York: Routledge.

Strike, K.A., Haller, E.J. & Soltis, J.F. (1998). *The ethics of school administration* (2nd ed.). New York: Teachers College Press.

Sullivan, W.M. (1982). *Reconstructing public philosophy*. Berkeley, CA: University of California Press.

Swimme, B. & Berry, T. (1992). *The universe story*. San Francisco: Harper.

Taylor, C. (1992). *The ethics of authenticity*. Cambridge, MA: Harvard University Press.

Tuana, N. (2007). Conceptualising moral literacy. *Journal of Educational Administration, 45*(4), 364–378.

Turiel, E. (2002). *The culture of morality: Social development, context, and conflict*. New York: Cambridge University Press.

Wall, J. (2010). *Ethics in the light of childhood*. Washington, DC: Georgetown University Press.

Whitehead, A.N. (1957). *Process and reality: An essay in cosmology*. New York: Free Press.

Whitehead, A.N. (1957). *The aims of education and other essays*. New York: Free Press.

Wiles, M. (1983). *Children into pupils*. London: Routledge and Kegan Paul.

Wiske, M.S. (Ed.) (1998). *Teaching for understanding: Linking research with practice*. San Francisco: Jossey Bass.

Wood, G.H. (1998). *A time to learn.* New York: Dutton.

Young, R. (1990). *A critical theory of education.* New York: Teachers College Press.

Zaretsky, L. (2005). Enacting democratic ethical educational leadership: Moving beyond the talk. Paper delivered at the University Council of Educational Administration (UCEA) Convention, Nashville, Tennessee, November 11–14.

Zehr, H. (2002). *The little book of restorative justice.* Intercourse, PA: Good Books.

Zohar, D. & Marshall, I. (1994). *The quantum society: Mind, physics, and a new social vision.* London: Harper Collins.

Index

individualism 40, 98
intimacy 77–8

justice. *See* ethic of justice

Kelcourse, F.B. x–xi
knowledge: ethical uses of 101–2, 105; internalization of 111–13; as object "out there" 102–3, 110–11; relationality of 99–100, 103–5; as respectful 100–1. *See also* learning
knowledge economy 8, 131
Kohlberg, Lawrence 37, 40–1, 59–61
Kurtines, M. 57

Langlois, L. 60–1
Lapointe, C. 60–1
"Leaders Transforming Learning and Learners" (LTLL) 147–56
learners: dialogical relationship with curriculum 117–19, 118f; moral agenda of 92–3; private vs. public selves of 93–4; relevancy of learning to 119, 130, 136–7, 142–3; teachers' relationship with 115–17, 115f; and virtue of presence 121–2
learning: as banking process, in traditional pedagogy 15–16, 102–3; as contextual 99–100; as dialogical 112, 114; and the Ego 82–4, 83f; the good of 109; inauthenticity of traditional 85–6, 96; internalization of 118–19; narrative vs. formal types of 84–5; relationality as basis of meaningful 94–5; relevancy to learners 119, 130, 136–7, 142–3; teachers as cultivators of 109–10; types of, necessary for 21st-century 113; and virtue of authenticity 122–3; and virtue of responsibility 123–4. *See also* knowledge
learning outcomes 133–7
learning theory 133–7, 155
Levine, C. 69
love 37, 58, 158. *See also* ethic of care
LTLL. *See* "Leaders Transforming Learning and Learners" (LTLL)

Macintyre, A. 109
mass media 6–7
material reality 10–11, 44–5
Mawhinney, H.B. 6
meaning. *See* relevancy
membership: conscience of 29; in daily life 45–6; use of term 20–1; and virtue of authenticity 122–3. *See also* relationality

mission statement 128–31
modernity, early: individualism as flaw of 98; science as foundation of 11–13
modernity, reflexive: Beck on need for 13–14; definition of 14
moral, use of term viii
moral development: academic curriculum as vehicle for 95–7, 105–6; culture as variable in 64; and gender 22, 37, 60–1, 65–6; and identity formation 61–5; maturity of 66–7; psychology of 58–61; schools' disregard of 97; as situated within larger field of human development 57; vs. social conventions 67; of women and girls 37, 58, 60. *See also* Erikson's model of human development; identity; pre-ethical development
mothers 65–6

Nucci, Larry 64
Nussbaum, Martha 161n2

obedience 61–3
organizational structure 139

parents 137–8
pedagogy: as dialogical 118f; effect of, on learners' authenticity 96–7; as guided by learning theory 133, 155; presence and authenticity in 123; teacher's reflection on 120; traditional vs. relational methods of 14–17
philosophy ix, 11, 49, 56–7
Piaget, Jean 58–9, 84
pre-ethical development viii, xiii, 57, 77, 91
presence 121–2
professional development 120
psychology of moral development 58–61

Rawls, John 40, 56
reality. *See* material reality
reciprocity 61–3
relationality: and autonomy 24–5, 32; as basis of meaningful learning 94–5; in daily life 46; effect on education 10–11; in Erikson's model of human development 74–5, 77–8; and essence of reality 44–5; and ethic of care 36–8; and ethics 20–1; and gender 46–7; of human development 20; of knowledge 99–101, 103–5; of school, home, and community 137–8
relevancy 119, 130, 136, 142–3
responsibility 123–4